DATE DUE

Pasold Studies in Textile History 6

Technology and Enterprise

The Pasold Research Fund

The Pasold Research Fund's field of interest covers the study of the history of textiles in all their respects — embracing the economic and social history of textiles, their technological development, design, conservation, the history of dress and other uses of textiles. The Fund was established in 1964 by the late Eric W. Pasold OBE, who had a special interest in the history of knitting, and its work was developed and extended by the late Kenneth G. Ponting as Research Director from 1967 to 1983. Negley Harte, Senior Lecturer in Economic History at University College London, is now the Director.

In addition to providing grants for research and organising conferences, the Fund sponsors the journal *Textile History* which appears twice a year and other publications.

Pasold Studies in Textile History

1 European Textile Printers in the Eighteenth Century: A Study of Peel and Oberkampf
   S.D. Chapman and S. Chassagne

2 Cloth and Clothing in Medieval Europe: Essays in Memory of Professor E.M. Carus-Wilson
   edited by N.B. Harte and K.G. Ponting

3 The British Wool Textile Industry, 1770–1914
   K.G. Ponting and D.T. Jenkins

4 Medieval English Clothmaking: An Economic Survey
   A.R. Bridbury

5 The East Anglian Linen Industry: Rural Industry and Local Economy, 1500–1850
   Nesta Evans

6 Technology and Enterprise: Isaac Holden and the Mechanisation of Woolcombing in France, 1848–1914
   Katrina Honeyman and Jordan Goodman

7 The Dress of the Venetians, 1495–1525
   Stella Mary Newton

Pasold Studies in Textile History 6

Technology and Enterprise

Isaac Holden and the Mechanisation of Woolcombing in France, 1848–1914

Katrina Honeyman
and
Jordan Goodman

Scolar
Press
The Pasold Research Fund

Published by
Scolar Press
Gower House
Croft Road
Aldershot
Hants GU11 3HR
England

Gower Publishing Company
Old Post Road
Brookfield
Vermont 05036
USA

British Library Cataloguing in Publication Data

Honeyman, Katrina
    Technology and enterprise: Isaac Holden
    and the mechanisation of woolcombing in
    France, 1848-1914.—(Pasold studies in
    textile history; 6)
1. Wool trade and industry—France—
    Technological innovations—History
    I. Title   II. Goodman, Jordan   III. Series
    338.4'767731'0944   11D9902.5

    ISBN 0 85967 727 3

Printed in Great Britain at the
University Press, Cambridge

Contents

List of Tables and Figures

List of Illustrations

Acknowledgements

This study would not have been possible without the help of a number of people to whom we should like to express our gratitude. Thanks are due to Sir Edward Holden for leading us to documents in the possession of members of his family, particularly Mrs Annie M. Bywater and her daughter Annette Bywater. They kindly invited us to consult papers of theirs concerning Isaac Holden's business, and put us in touch with other descendants of his. One of these, Miss Janet Gough, allowed us access to her rich collection of financial records of Holden's French factories, which provided much of the information contained in Chapters 4 and 5.

We should also like to thank the Librarian and Archivist at the Brotherton Library, University of Leeds and the J.B. Priestley Library, University of Bradford who made available to us their large collection of papers on the business and inventive activities of Isaac Holden. During our researches in France, the Archivists in Châlons-sur-Marne and in Lille were particularly helpful.

Finally, we wish to acknowledge the generous assistance of the British Academy, whose financial support enabled us to undertake research in France.

Abbreviations

Archives

France

AN	Archives Nationales
ADM	Archives Departementales de la Marne
ADN	Archives Departementales du Nord
ADS	Archives Departementales de la Seine
AMC	Archives Municipales de Croix
AMR	Archives Municipales de Roubaix
AMSD	Archives Municipales de St Denis

England

B	Holden Papers, University of Bradford
L	Holden Business Archive, University of Leeds
G	Private papers held by Miss Janet Gough, London
By	Private papers held by Mrs Annie M. Bywater, East Grinstead, Sussex

Printed material

HIL	F. Byles and A.J. Best, *The Holden-Illingworth Letters* (Bradford, 1927)

Figure 1: France (showing main places mentioned in text)

1 Introduction

This case study serves both a specific and a general purpose. It focuses on the technical and industrial changes associated with the mechanisation of the woolcombing sector of the French worsted industry during the second half of the nineteenth century. Isaac Holden, a prominent English inventor and businessman, played a crucial role in this process, and it is largely through a detailed examination of his technical and commercial exploits in France that this study unfolds. The issues raised in the course of the book, however, have broader implications for our understanding of the nature of European industrialisation during this period. Two problems receive particular attention: the nature of innovations and technical choice; and the relationship between technology and industrial organisation.

It is often believed that in the early stages of industrialisation, when the technical gap between European economies was large, the process of technological change within an economy typically took the form of an indigenously-developed technology improved by relatively advanced, imported techniques. By this means, the discrepancies of technical achievement among European economies were gradually eroded; and it was from the middle of the nineteenth century that technical development became increasingly based on indigenous invention. This progression was the result of a levelling of expertise acting in response to the growing protectionism – in the form of patent laws – surrounding the diffusion process.

It is generally agreed that European industrialisation spread by means of the diffusion of technology. Sidney Pollard, an effective exponent of this view, writes that 'the essential core of the process [of industrialisation]…was technological…the process started in Britain and the industrialisation of Europe took place on the British model; it was, as far as the Continent was concerned, a purely and deliberately imitative process.'[1] The notion that technical changes emanated from Britain and were then emulated by European economies is also emphasised by David Landes.[2] The diffusion process, initially at least, was facilitated by the movement of people.[3] W. O. Henderson shows how inventors, entrepreneurs and skilled workmen took the latest British manufacturing techniques across the Channel to France, Belgium, Germany and other European economies from the late eighteenth to the late nineteenth centuries, irrespective of potentially restricting legislation.[4] David Jeremy, in his study of the diffusion of technology from Britain to the United States in the eighteenth and early nineteenth centuries, has convincingly shown the importance of the migration of skilled workers between the two countries in this process.[5] It should be emphasised, however, that other European economies, from an early stage, similarly exported their technical expertise and developments. Rondo Cameron devotes a book to the role of the French in European industrialisation; and John McKay's book on Russian industrial development highlights the importance of Belgian and French entrepreneurs and work people.[6]

Despite the variety of technologies transmitted and the diversity of economic structures involved in the diffusion process, there are just two categories typically referred to by writers on the subject within which the whole experience of technical transfer falls. First, technologies were diffused – with or without adaptations by the receiving firms or economies – in response to different economic, social and cultural conditions. In the second case, technologies were actively or even strenuously diffused, either because of the willingness of the innovator to spread the new technology (Richard Roberts' self-acting mule, and Bessemer and his convertor are examples), or because of the strong desire of the receiver to take possession of the latest technology.

This interpretation implies that the process was uniformly positive, and that technological diffusion was relatively simple and speedy. For a more complete understanding of the mechanism of the spread of innovations, however, it is important to know which technologies were not successfully transmitted despite willingness on both sides; and which technologies were deliberately prevented from general diffusion. This aspect is seldom investigated.

A further defect in the prevailing body of thinking on the subject is its tendency to assume (admittedly on the basis of much empirical work) that the diffusion of technique typically took place from a more technically advanced to a less advanced economy. This view is entirely consistent with the 'positive' interpretation of technological diffusion. When economies are at similar levels of technical advancement, however, as in Europe in the later nineteenth century, then the more restrictive aspects of diffusion, reflected in the legalised protection of technology and the prevention of transmission, are likely to undermine the positive or permissive features of the process. When examining late nineteenth-century technical change in Europe, therefore, because the core industrial economies – Germany, France, Belgium and Britain – were at similar technical levels, it should be as fruitful to focus on the protection of technology and the response of other economies to this, as on the ease of the diffusion process.

Once patent legislation had matured to the stage that the protection of an invention was internationally applicable, the way was open for technical innovations to be treated as a monopolistic tool.[7] Largely for reasons of timing, it was the chemical, electrical, special metal and communications industries of the late nineteenth century that first employed patent laws to ensure a monopoly, not only over technology but also over the process of invention, thus achieving a major share of the market.

S. B. Saul has drawn attention to the importance of the patent in the late nineteenth century and has cited several interesting examples of the way in which patents were used both to diffuse and to protect technology. His examples also indicate the response of economies to the suppression of the diffusion of technology.[8] Pursuing a different historical problem, David Noble has also focused on the role of patents and has shown convincingly how restricted access to technology through patent purchases underpinned the structure of corporate capitalism which formed the organising principle of late nineteenth-century, science-based American industry.[9]

The literature on technical change in the late nineteenth century, therefore, is typically concerned, either implicitly or explicitly, with the safeguarding rather than the diffusion of technology.[10] As such, it more accurately represents the nature of technical diffusion than works on the earlier period; and probably reflects real changes taking place in the role of the patent from a transmitter to a protector of technical development during the nineteenth century. The new role of the patent, however, while protectionist, was by no means wholly restrictive; and from the middle of the nineteenth century, the sale of patent rights became an increasingly important element within the process of technical diffusion.

In this study of the mechanisation of woolcombing in France during the second half of the nineteenth century, the focus is on the nature and effects of the constraints placed upon the diffusion of technology, by Isaac Holden's inventive and business activities. Within the context of the dynamic role of the patent in technical change, this study clearly illustrates the fate of inventions emerging when control over the diffusion of technology was changing.

This study also confronts the general issue of the relationship between technology and industrial organisation. The close examination of the mechanisation of woolcombing clearly reveals the intimacy of that relationship. In particular, it shows that technical innovations in woolcombing were conceived of and developed within specific industrial organisations and that this profoundly influenced the nature of the diffusion of this technology. Moreover, it contributed significantly to the dramatic growth in the scale of enterprise and the concentration of production, both of which featured largely in general

European industrial development in the second half of the nineteenth century.

The discovery of a commercially viable and workable woolcombing technique was a protracted process and its eventual appearance coincided with both the development of capital goods industries and the sharp change in the way in which patents were used in the diffusion process. It therefore marks the end of the period of major technical advance in consumer goods industries when diffusion was primarily permissive, and the beginning of the period when the patent was used as a protectionist tool. It is usual to associate changes in patent legislation and patent use with the more sophisticated technology of the capital goods industries and the science-based industries. This study suggests that the type of industry was less important than the timing of its move into modern techniques of production when discussing manipulation of the patent system.

Combing is an essential process in the manufacture of worsted yarn, which distinguishes it from woollen production. The purpose of combing is to separate the short 'noil' fibres from the longer 'top' fibres in the raw wool. The noil is then discarded and the longer fibres are combined in a parallel arrangement to form a sliver which, after further treatment, is spun into worsted yarn. The characteristic strength and softness of worsted yarn and cloth is thus achieved by the working in parallel of fibres of equal length.

Attempts to mechanise the combing stage of worsted manufacture began in the late eighteenth century when the productive processes of a number of textile industries were revolutionised by a series of fundamental technical changes. Combing, however, proved particularly unyielding to mechanical solution; and the frustrating search for a solution continued, mainly in Britain and France, throughout most of the first half of the nineteenth century. Handcombing was still predominant in both countries late in the 1840s, by which time a technical breakthrough was imminent. Between 1845 and 1850, the machine combs of Josué Heilmann (an Alsatian machine-maker) and Isaac Holden and Samuel Cunliffe Lister emerged independently and were patented.

Isaac Holden, businessman and inventor, left England in 1849, at the age of 42, to open a woolcombing factory in France on the basis of a partnership with Samuel Cunliffe Lister (later Lord Masham), who remained in England. Premises were procured at St Denis on the outskirts of Paris, and Holden began to supply the French worsted industry with mechanically-combed wool, using their invention, the Square Motion machine comb first patented in 1847.

For Holden and Lister, as for earlier immigrant industrialists, Continental Europe provided a natural and lucrative extension of their interests and enterprises. In opening their factory in France, they followed a tradition of British entrepreneurial activities. Yet the particular experience of the two men was unusual. The motivating force behind their relocation was not the international technological gap which had typically instigated previous migrations from Britain beginning in the late eighteenth century, but rather the unequivocal desire to dominate French woolcombing by impeding the diffusion of competing technologies – both English and French. This they intended to do by restricting the transformation of competing ideas into machines, and by appropriating a large proportion of the French market with combed wool produced on their own machine.

Prior to the formation of their partnership, Holden and Lister had independently become interested in woolcombing technology; each had practical experience in English worsted production and each was familiar with the conditions of the French industry. Otherwise, they had little in common and had reached their positions from quite different origins.[11]

Holden's background was comparatively humble and he followed a lengthy route to wealth and status. After several unsatisfying occupations, Holden, who was nurturing an inventive spirit, secured a position as a bookkeeper in a worsted mill near Bradford. Here he quickly acquired some mechanical expertise and commercial instinct. After sixteen years at the mill in a semi-managerial position, he quit following a disagreement with his employers and established a small and singularly unsuccessful worsted factory in Bradford.

Samuel Cunliffe Lister's pedigree, by contrast, was long and illustrious. He had been placed in the expanding Bradford worsted industry at the age of 23 in 1838, when his father, a substantial landowner, built Manningham Mills for his two sons. Lister's advantages of birth were enhanced by his clear talent, and by the 1840s, he had not only enticed some of the leading technical minds into his employ and headed one of the largest worsted mills in the West Riding, but he was harbouring plans for expansion both in Yorkshire and on the Continent of Europe.

The partnership between the two men was thus an uneasy compromise between backgrounds and aspirations – which ultimately proved unworkable – but it did lay the basis of a quite remarkable business. By 1858, when the partnership ended and Holden purchased Lister's share in the business, two factories, one in Reims and one in Croix, had been added to the original mill in St Denis. Together with his nephews, Jonathan Holden and Isaac Crothers, as managing partners, Holden took the French worsted industry by storm and influenced the course of woolcombing there for the rest of the century.

The organisation of this work reflects the course of Holden's achievements as an inventor and as a specialist comber in France. Chapter 2 outlines the technical history of woolcombing before the middle of the nineteenth century, and ascribes reasons for the high failure rate of attempts to perfect the machine comb. The concluding sections of the chapter examine in detail the work of those inventors who eventually succeeded in producing workable machine combs: Josué Heilmann, Isaac Holden and Samuel Cunliffe Lister.

Chapter 3 focuses on the years of Lister and Holden's partnership in France when, as a result of their joint efforts in purchasing and suppressing rival woolcombing patents, they were to dominate the technical side of the industry. Chapter 4 examines the establishment of the partners' manufacturing activities in France and follows the fortunes of their first factory in St Denis. Chapter 5 continues to look at the success of the enterprise by examining the performance of the main factories in Croix and Reims from their establishment in the early 1850s until the end of the century. Chapter 6 discusses Holden's entrepreneurial qualities and the difficulties and problems he encountered in the management of his extensive enterprise. Chapter 7 provides an assessment of Holden's role in the diffusion of woolcombing technology in France. The discussion is then broadened to include the organisation of woolcombing production which was closely related to the technical changes occurring and where Holden's influence was equally important.

The sources on which this study is based can usefully be divided into two categories: those that relate directly to Holden, his partnership, his business and his patent activities; and those that illuminate his influence on the diffusion of woolcombing technology in France. In the first category, the documents consist of letters written to Holden – chiefly by Lister, Jonathan Holden and Isaac Crothers; and various factory records such as annual balance sheets and cost accounts (including figures of output, operating costs and profits). The account books have not survived.

The nature of this documentation imposes certain constraints and introduces possible bias. It is impossible, for instance, to provide a complete account of the operations of Holden's factories in France, because only a small proportion of the relevant decisions taken and problems faced by the managers are discussed in the letters. The analysis, therefore, focuses on the protection of technology which forms a major part of the information available. Secondly, because the factories' accounts do not exist, it is impossible to obtain a clear picture of Holden's business network in France. This gap in our knowledge precludes a full assessment of Holden's role in woolcombing in France. Despite these restrictions, however, the documentation on Holden is rich and rewarding.

The sources within the second category are mostly contained in French archives. Plentiful information can be usefully extracted from voluminous, regular reports on the state of the industry, including levels of output, productivity and profit rates, filed by the prefects and sub-prefects of the French *départements*. Much of the evidence in Chapter 5 is derived from such reports. It is, however, impossible to provide a complete perspective on Holden as a manufacturer, because of the dearth of business records; but the official sources allow a broad comparison to be made between Holden and his rivals in Reims and Roubaix with respect to the size, structure and organisation of their firms.

The restrictions imposed by the data, together with a desire to do justice to the question of technical change, have prevented a full discussion of closely-related themes upon which this study touches. The two most important themes are the nature of nineteenth-century French industrialisation; and the history of French labour. The justification for their exclusion is set out below.

The subject of the French worsted industry is pursued in this study only to the extent that it is germane to the general theme of technical change and diffusion. There is no doubt that the French worsted industry in the nineteenth century typifies many of the general characteristics of French industrial development.[12] The lack of concentration, for instance, the relatively slow pace of technical change and the prolonged coexistence of different organisations of production were all experienced in conjunction with reasonably rapid rates of growth.[13] These aspects, while important, are raised in this study only when they aid an understanding of the course of technical change in woolcombing or highlight Holden's particular actions with respect to factory location or choice of technology. The French worsted industry and its relationship to the pattern of French industrialisation deserves a separate study.

Equally, this study cannot do full justice to the subject of labour history which, in recent years especially, has done much to deepen our understanding of the social, economic and political development of nineteenth-century France.[14] Holden's factories in Croix and Reims were amongst the largest in the country, and consequently the problems of coordination, discipline, recruitment and organisation were enormous. This important aspect of Holden's enterprise requires a separate study. To pursue it here in any depth, would be to detract from this book's main objective.

The purpose of this book, therefore, is precise if modest. It aims to clarify the mechanism by which the diffusion of a particular technology was constrained by legislation and individual action, and the effect this had on the evolution of a single industry. Even in its modest objective, however, this book hopes to shed light on a variety of important and general issues concerning technological change and the process of industrialisation in the second half of the nineteenth century.

Notes

1   S. Pollard, *Peaceful Conquest: The Industrialisation of Europe, 1760–1970* (Oxford, 1981), p. v. Views to the contrary have been expressed. See note 12 below.

2   D. Landes, *The Unbound Prometheus* (Cambridge, 1969).

3   In the words of one economic historian: 'apart from some striking cases of imitation, the diffusion of technology in the modern world has been largely limited by techniques not unfamiliar to St Paul or Mohammed: the movement of persons and the transmittal of written documents.' W. Parker, 'Economic Development in Historical Perspective', *Economic Development and Cultural Change*, October 1961, p. 1. The work of Nathan Rosenberg on technology and its diffusion has considerably influenced historical studies in the field. See his collection of important essays *Perspectives on Technology* (Cambridge, 1976) and *Inside the Black Box* (Cambridge, 1983).

4   W. O. Henderson, *Britain and Industrial Europe, 1750–1870* (Leicester, 1972). D. J. Jeremy, 'Damming the Flood: British Government Efforts to Check the Outflow of Technicians and Machinery, 1780–1843', *Business History Review*, 51, (1977), pp. 1–34. Similar observations have been made about the diffusion of technology in the early modern period. See for example, C. M. Cipolla, 'The Diffusion of Innovations in Early Modern Europe', *Comparative Studies in Society and History*, 14 (1972), pp. 46–52; D. C. Coleman, 'An Innovation and its Diffusion: the "New Draperies"', *Economic History Review*, 12 (1969), pp. 417–29; J. Clayburn la Force, 'Technological Diffusion in the Eighteenth Century: the Spanish Textile Industry', *Technology and Culture*, 5 (1964) pp. 322–43; W. C. Scoville, 'Minority Migrations and the Diffusion of Technology', *Journal of Economic History*, 11 (1951), pp. 347–60; 'The Huguenots and the Diffusion of Technology', *Journal of Political Economy*, 60 (1952), pp. 294–311, 392–411.

5   D. J. Jeremy, *Transatlantic Industrial Revolution: The Diffusion of Textile Technologies Between Britain and America, 1790–1830s* (Oxford, 1981).

6   R. E. Cameron, *France and the Economic Development of Europe, 1800–1914* (Princeton, 1961); J. P. McKay, *Pioneers for Profit* (Chicago, 1970).

7   For the use and abuse of patents generally, see F. L. Vaughan, 'Patent Policy', *American Economic Review: Papers and Proceedings*, 38 (1948), pp. 215–34; E. Penrose, *The Economics of the International Patent System* (Baltimore, 1951); and N. Rosenberg (ed.), *The Economics of Technological Change* (Harmondsworth, 1971).

8   S. B. Saul, 'The Nature and Diffusion of Technology', in A. J. Youngson, *Economic Development in the Long Run* (London, 1972), pp. 55–7.

9   D. Noble, *America by Design* (Oxford, 1979).

10 Landes, *Unbound Prometheus*, pp. 269–76; A. S. Milward and S. B. Saul, *The Economic Development of Continental Europe, 1780–1870* (London, 1979), pp. 171–247.

11 Biographical information on Holden can be found in Chapter 2 and Epilogue, this volume; and E. Jennings, 'Sir Isaac Holden (1807–1897):

"The First Comber in Europe"', Ph. D. University of Bradford, 1982. For Lister, see *Dictionary of National Biography*, 2nd supplement, 2 (1912), pp. 469-70; S. Cunliffe Lister, *Days of Yore: A History of Masham* (unpublished, 1978); H. L. Lyster Denny, *Memorials of an Ancient House: A History of Lister or Lyster* (Edinburgh, 1913); and Lister's autobiography, *Lord Masham's Inventions: Written by Himself* (London, 1905); and Epilogue, this volume.

12 See for example, F. Crouzet, 'French Economic Growth in the Nineteenth Century Reconsidered', *History*, 59 (1974), pp. 167-79; R. Roehl, 'French Industrialization: A Reconsideration', *Explorations in Economic History*, 13 (1976), pp. 233-81; P. O'Brien and C. Keyder, *Economic Growth in Britain and France, 1780-1914* (London, 1978); and the most recent survey, R. Cameron and C. E. Freedman, 'French Economic Growth: A Radical Revision', *Social Science History*, 7 (1983), pp. 3-30.

13 On the basis of the size of its spinning sector, the French worsted industry grew rapidly during the nineteenth century and was, for most of the second half of the century, not far behind Britain, its main rival. By the time of the outbreak of World War I, France was probably just holding third place in the international league of worsted producers having lost ground to the United States. (Total worsted spinning capacity *c.* 1910-13 Britain 2.938 million spindles; United States 2.624 million spindles; Germany 2.364 million spindles.) The changes in France's worsted spinning capacity can be seen from the following table.

Table 1.1: Worsted spinning capacity in France, 1815-1913

	Number of spindles
1815	Negligible
1829	240,000
1844	600,000
1847	750,000
1851	850,000
1862	1,300,000
1867	1,750,000
1878	2,270,000
1894	2,189,180
1910	1,994,000
1913	2,366,000

Sources: For comparative data, Committee on Industry and Trade, *Survey of Industries* (London, 1928), Part III, p. 242-56; P. T. Cherington, *The Wool Industry* (New York, 1916), p. 9. For France, chronologically (up to and including 1851): *Exposition universelle de 1851: Travaux de la commission française* (Paris, 1854), vol. 4, p. 155; *Exposition universelle de 1867 à Paris: Rapports du Jury International* (Paris, 1868), vol. 4, p. 114; A. Picard, *Le Bilan d'un siècle, 1801-1900* (Paris, 1906), vol. 4, p. 352; *Annuaire Statistique de la France*, vol. 16, pp. 288-9; Ministère du commerce, de l'industrie, des postes etc., *Rapport général sur l'industrie française sa situation son avenir* (Paris, 1919), vol. 1, p. 359; Committee on Trade and Industry, *Survey*, p. 243.

14 See for example the pioneering work by M. Perrot, *Les ouvriers en grève*, 2 vols (Paris, 1974).

2 Woolcombing Technology: The State of the Art to 1850

As late as 1845, the problem of mechanical combing had not been completely resolved, yet the economic advantages of such a machine had been apparent since the late eighteenth century when the first technique was patented by Edmund Cartwright. Between 1790 and 1845, inventors, mechanics and entrepreneurs on both sides of the Channel directed their attention to the woolcombing issue. Developments during this period typically constituted improvements upon the principles contained in Cartwright's patents.

The technical gap to be bridged by a machine comb was enormous. The inventors were seeking to replicate the action of the handcomber; there was no intermediate stage, no 'machine' (such as a loom) that required only to be mechanised. For more than 50 years inventors worked with increasing urgency, yet with growing optimism as each subsequent machine removed the technical and operational defects of its predecessors. As success drew near, from the early 1840s, patented inventions proliferated, and by the 1850s, several commercially viable machines had emerged. While initially in competition, the complementarity of these machines was soon evident. Each machine served a slightly different purpose and provided a varied package of benefits for the manufacturer. The choice of a particular machine for commercial application was the result of the manufacturer's perception of his needs, the type of raw material used, the required quality of the finished product, and the level of skill of the labour force.

The development of a fully operational machine comb was a prolonged process when seen in the context of technical innovations elsewhere in the textile industry. Its history is both interesting and vital for an understanding of the progress of the worsted industry during the nineteenth century.

The first machine comb to be patented, in 1789, was that of Edmund Cartwright, perhaps better remembered as the inventor of the power loom.[1] His two subsequent patents (1790 and 1792) improved upon the first; and the third, popularly known as 'Big Ben', achieved a limited commercial application for coarse wools.[2] This comb, however, was more significant for the influence it had on subsequent inventions; the principles of the early Cartwright machine could still be observed 60 years later.[3]

The combing process that Cartwright was the first to reproduce mechanically comprised three principal stages – filling, combing and drawing off – and until the 1840s, handcombers fulfilled these functions better than any existing machine. On the introduction of his own machine, however, Cartwright had declared that 'machine-combed wool is better, especially for machine spinning, by at least 12 per cent being all equally mixed and the slivers uniform and of any required length.'[4] Certainly, the potential gains to be achieved by the worsted manufacturers from machine combing, partially realised by Cartwright's inventions, were enormous. Inventive activity, initially more marked in England than in France, was first encouraged by the justifiable expectation of reward, and then further stimulated when the emergence of a marketable machine comb seemed imminent.[5]

In 1805, James Noble, in the first of several contributions to wool-combing development, patented a pre-combing machine with a travelling carriage, moving backwards and forwards, separating top from noil.[6] Of less lasting significance was George Gilpin's 1811 patent for a machine to comb and prepare wool. His invention's peculiar motion, attributable to the elliptical cog wheels, was not adopted in any later patent.[7]

During the next 25 years, the most significant advances in wool-combing technology were made in France. The first such patent was taken out in 1814 by James Collier, an English expatriot entrepreneur. He had established several spinning concerns in various parts of France and, while in business in Paris, became interested in the woolcombing problem. His proposed solution took the form of a machine designed to separate each fibre for combing, and he initiated the use of steam for those fibres that required heat, or heat and oil for successful combing. The design never achieved practical application, and James Collier returned to England in 1814 to pursue his business career.[8] John Collier, James' younger brother, however, contributed much more enduringly to the mechanical combing of wool. As a young engineer, he migrated to France and established a machine-making business in Paris. He too became fascinated by the elusiveness of a machine comb and determined to develop one.[9]

Despite the activities of the English brothers, the first French machine was built in 1826 by J.-B. Godard, an Amiens mechanic.[10] He sold the patent rights of his technique to John Collier, who subsequently perfected the idea. Collier patented his improved version in 1827 jointly with John Platt, a Salford machine-maker, and continued to exploit it with further improvements, until his death ten years later.[11] His widow, Juliana, then supervised its construction and diffusion from factory premises in St Denis on the outskirts of Paris. The 1827 advance was significant as it developed the principle of combing between two circular combs, to each of which was attached a pair of drawing-off rollers.[12] It was by no means perfect, however, and although it dealt adequately with coarse material, it produced large amounts of noil and insufficiently combed the middle portion of the fibre.[13] Despite its shortcomings, the Collier comb was the most successful woolcombing technology in France until the late 1840s.[14]

Because John Collier's comb clearly brought the problem of mechanical combing close to a resolution, the activity of other inventors accelerated. The specifications of the French patents until the mid-1840s show that most combing developments in France from 1826 concentrated upon the improvement of the Collier comb.[15]

In England, meanwhile, the output of machine combs was more diverse in technical and inventive origin, but the success rate was no greater.[16] Between 1830 and 1845, four Englishmen contributed substantively and independently to the realisation of a viable combing machine. James Noble and George Edmund Donisthorpe each patented small improvements to existing machines during the 1830s, and while not completely successful, the innovations contained valid principles.[17]

Another Englishman, Isaac Holden, was also devoting much time and energy to the woolcombing problem during the 1830s. Of those so far mentioned, Holden was perhaps the least likely to become involved in these complex technical problems, having followed a career outside the industry.[18] The son of a coalmine foreman, Isaac Holden spent his childhood and adolescence in Scotland, receiving a good, well-rounded education. Much of it, however, was on a part-time basis alternating between work as a draw-boy and a piecer at a cotton factory and school.

Holden seemed destined for a teaching career. In 1827, aged 20, he took up a teaching post in Leeds after some years as a teaching assistant in Scotland, but for various reasons, his stay in Leeds was short.[19] After similarily short teaching appointments elsewhere, he returned to Scotland in 1830, determined to start a school of his own offering tuition in bookkeeping and other commercial skills.

Unfortunately, this plan did not come to fruition and it seemed that destiny was to follow another course. Holden made a momentous decision: he gave up teaching and accepted the post of bookkeeper for the worsted spinning firm of Townend Brothers, in Cullingworth near Keighley. Within a very short time, Holden seems to have become totally fascinated by the technical aspects of worsted production.[20] Characteristically, in his spare time, he devoted himself entirely to studying those subjects – mechanics, mechanical drawing and metal-lurgy, – most relevant to his current fascination. Townend Brothers recognised his drive and interest in textile technology, and in 1834, he visited the Paris Exhibition on the firm's behalf.[21] While in Paris, he acquainted himself with the main features of the French worsted industry and the merino wool trade, and, more importantly, took the opportunity of seeing the Collier comb in operation at the Exhibition and at Collier's own workshop.[22] So impressed was he with this machine, that within weeks of his return from France, Holden had persuaded his employers to install it in their Cullingworth mill. Unfortunately, however, the Collier comb performed erratically under the supervision of Townend, and, rather than jettison the project, Holden was made responsible for its operation. He experimented and improved upon it, and thenceforth became increasingly absorbed in its technology though none of his efforts produced anything that could be patented.[23]

While Holden was experimenting, George Donisthorpe, in 1842, patented a significant advance on his earlier efforts.[24] Although this revised machine operated substantially on Cartwright's principles, its special contribution lay in the particular arrangement of teeth on the comb; the teeth becoming progressively finer along the length of the comb bar.[25] The aim of this technique was that the major obstacles and impurities in the wool would initially be removed by the stronger and coarser teeth, preparing the fringe for treatment by the finer teeth. The working combs were given a rotary action to imitate the handcomber; and, to ease combing, these were treated by steam or hot water. Donisthorpe continued to work on this machine and patented several improvements in 1843.[26]

Before too long, Donisthorpe's activities attracted the attention of Samuel Cunliffe Lister. Lister was a substantial, highly established and influential worsted manufacturer in Bradford who became interested in the industrial exploitation of the machine comb. For several years the two men worked together, and in 1845, Lister patented a design that was essentially an operational improvement on Donisthorpe's original.[27] Lister replaced the rotary working combs by a simple sliding table, or 'gauntree', which carried a set of four working combs, and a spare set for use when the others were being cleaned. Although this machine was soon commercially adopted for the combing of fine wool, it was not entirely successful for two reasons. First, a number of fibres hung down the centre of the circular comb and were thereby missed by the teeth; and secondly, the longer hair tended to get trapped in the teeth.[28] The correction of these two defects, through the efforts of Lister and Holden, who joined forces in 1846, resulted in the Square Motion comb.[29] Noble and Donisthorpe temporarily pooled their resources in order to improve the Noble comb.[30] Within a few years, these four men, both singly and in various combinations, produced several competing machine combs that reached the level of commercial viability.

Two major obstacles had frustrated the success of the early (pre-1845) attempts to apply powered machinery to woolcombing. The serious problem of fibre breakage, particularly in the French worsted industry where the use of fine merino wool predominated, was coupled with that of an expensive loss of large quantities of long wool. Much of the top was combed into the waste product, noil, by the essentially clumsy early machines. Until 1845, therefore, the delicate nature of the raw material hindered mechanical solution, and the more dextrous handcombers, who wasted less long wool, thus remained the preferred alternative.[31] A quantitative assessment of the comparative efficiency of hand and machine combing was made by Isaac Holden. At the time of his trials in 1837, he discovered that although there was little difference between the two methods, handcombing was less wasteful and the product superior, but the output was about 9 per cent more expensive. Combing by the early machines gave a tear (ratio of top to noil) of 2.75:1, while that achieved through handcombing was 3.15:1.[32]

The sluggish diffusion of the early combing machines is not surprising given the very small cost advantage and the essentially superior hand method. In France, only the Collier comb made any impact on the industry, while in England no comb was widely distributed until the 1840s.[33] Collier had improved on the Godard machine in patents of 1833 and 1838, the year of his death. Within France, the comb was purchased and used mainly by worsted spinners rather than specialist combers, although a group of Parisian combers began small-scale experimentation from the 1840s.[34]

The earliest example of a Collier comb in commercial use was in 1838 at André Koechlin and Company's worsted mill at Mulhouse, and it seems to have enjoyed reasonable success.[35] Lachapelle and Levarlet, woollen and worsted spinners in Reims, gained a silver medal at the French national exhibition of 1839 for their entry of yarn produced on the Collier machine.[36] By 1841 there were sixteen machine combs recorded in the Fourmies/Le Cateau region, ten of which belonged to the integrated worsted mill of Paturle-Lupin;[37] and in 1843, Théophile Legrand, the prominent Fourmies worsted spinner, installed machine combs in his mill for the first time.[38] A further 127 machines were located in specialised combing establishments, distributed as follows: 59 in Paris, 50 in Reims and 18 in the Nord *département*.[39] Of the total of 70 combing establishments in France in the mid-1840s, only 10 or 12 made use of the embryonic technology.[40]

Although handcombing was marginally more productive than the early machines, both methods were vastly inferior to post-1845 machine combs. For instance, in Reims in 1854, the new machines recorded tears of 8:1, and ratios of 20:1 were achieved later in the century.[41]

Between 1840 and 1849, the number of patents taken out for machine combs in France and Britain was 13 and 21, respectively, more than double the total patent output of the entire pre-1840 period, which had produced only one satisfactorily workable machine.[42] New principles of mechanical woolcombing also evolved during this decade and the inventions of the 1840s onwards were of two basic types. One group can be categorised as 'Bradford combs', and were apparently inspired by Cartwright's 'Big Ben': the inventions of Lister, Holden, Donisthorpe and Noble, which dominated the history of combing in England, were of this type.[43] The second group was typified by the Heilmann comb which was used extensively in France, but, mainly for reasons of patent law, was never worked in England.[44] The technical antecedents of this machine are obscure but there is no doubt that they differed from the Bradford variety which was based on the replication of the hand-combing movement.[45]

Josué Heilmann had taken an early interest in manufacturing technology, and, following an apprenticeship and one year's employment at his parents' cotton-spinning factory at Mulhouse, he set up cotton spinning on his own account in 1818.[46] Several years later he became interested in mechanical weaving and developed a machine that was widely used in England.[47] A variety of inventions followed, and during the 1830s Heilmann's interest shifted from cotton, to silk, to velours, and only towards the end of his life did he focus upon the woolcombing problem.[48] It was in 1843, while employed by Nicolas Schlumberger at his spinning and machine-making factory, that Heilmann started working on the idea of a machine comb for wool, cotton and silk in association with J.-J. Bourcart.[49] Schlumberger financed the project and when the comb was operational, he adopted the machine and had it constructed in his Guebwiller machine workshop.[50] The Heilmann comb was hailed, especially in France, as a particularly ingenious device which removed the defects of earlier designs and achieved excellent results.[51] Although Heilmann himself appreciated the potentially long-term significance of his technique, he died in poverty, leaving Schlumberger, then patentee, to reap the reward.[52]

Heilmann's comb was initially conceived and used for the preparation of cotton, but it was so designed that small modifications permitted its application to all textiles.[53] Heilmann dismissed the Collier machine which, he believed, damaged the wool in the combing process,[54] and his aim was to replicate the action of women as they combed their long hair.[55] The combing mechanism of the Heilmann machine was thus fixed so that the ends of the fibres were gently combed first with more pressure exerted as the comb traversed the length of the wool. There were two combs, each with a circular movement which processed a length of wool at each turn. The alternate action of the two combs, moving at different speeds, allowed the intermittent and progressive combing of the wool, which achieved the gentle action on the ends of the fibres. The original design accomplished a particular purity of product with very little waste.[56]

For the machine to operate optimally, a pre-combing stage was required. This reduced the pressure on the combs and minimised the damage to the slivers. The machine's action of separating the slivers ensured that each length of wool was combed evenly from one end to the other.[57] This was an important advance on earlier machines which had tended to leave the middle portion uncombed.[58] The Heilmann comb could be adapted for use with all types of wool; but it operated best on the short, fine, merino wool fibres which predominated in the French worsted industry.[59]

Although the inspiration for Heilmann's invention has been romanticised, it is clear that it was based on an entirely new principle rather than an improvement on earlier forms of machine combs. As such, it marked a new stage in the development of the machine comb, and after 1845, much expertise was directed towards the improvement of the Heilmann comb.[60]

It is interesting to note that while Heilmann was developing his apparently original and complex machine, Lister and Donisthorpe invented a similar means of combing wool mechanically. Consequently, Heilmann is believed to be the inventor of the 'Nip' principle in France and Germany, while in England, Lister and Donisthorpe are considered to have independently and earlier conceived an equivalent idea.[61] Whether or not the two designs evolved separately, Heilmann was the first to patent the device. The English patent was taken out in 1846, but, despite the undoubted value of the machine, the cost of protecting it in the early years exceeded the financial gains. Indeed, the heavy burden of litigation against infringers and supposed infringers of his patent led Heilmann into penury.[62] The most extensive legal battle, however, took place after his death, when his representative proceeded against Lister and Donisthorpe for patent infringement and obtained a verdict.[63] The rights to Heilmann's English patent were then sold to Akroyd and Salt for £30,000 who quickly resold to Lister for the same sum, retaining several machines for their own use. Lister's sole purpose in purchasing the rights to Heilmann's machine was to prevent its adoption in England.[64] He was entirely successful in this aim, and while the Heilmann machine was used widely in France and Germany, it was never adopted in England for the purpose of combing wool. It did, however, enjoy a limited application in cotton and flax production.[65] It seemed that English worsted manufacturers believed Lister's machine to be superior, and even after the expiration of Heilmann's patent, Lister still received £1000 for each of his own combs sold.[66]

While this episode reflects the rapidity with which commercially viable woolcombing machines emerged following the solution of previously intractable technical problems, it also reveals the practice of monopolising new technology through the purchase of competing patents. This novel tactic, which was later adopted in other industries, enabled the large manufacturer to determine the technical direction of the industry by purchasing and controlling all relevant patents, both complementary and competitive. It was in this activity that Samuel Cunliffe Lister's special genius lay:[67] and he was without doubt its most imaginative and successful exponent, on both sides of the Channel. In 1842 he had perceived that the perfection of a mechanical combing device would be highly lucrative, as both worsted and cotton manufacturers were anxious to replace the expensive handcombing process.[68] Lister's first purchase was a 50 per cent share in Donisthorpe's 1842 patent. Then, employing Donisthorpe under contract as his mechanic and using his ideas and expertise, Lister took out several patents in his name only between 1844 and 1848, and two more in their joint names in 1849 and 1850.[69] During the 1840s, while both men were developing the 'Nip' machine comb, Lister displayed his talent for dealing with potential competitors when he disposed of rival claims by legal action of infringements and patent purchases. Without any effective competition, the 'Nip' was successfully perfected (introducing an original feeding apparatus) and patented in 1851.[70] By 1853, in his single-minded aim to dominate wool-combing technology, Lister was in possession of 23 English patents – probably a complete collection of those relating to combing in the country.[71]

While exploiting Donisthorpe's inventive acumen, Lister also became associated with Isaac Holden.[72] Holden's considerable natural and acquired talents were consistently undervalued by his employers, who refused Holden's request for a well-deserved partnership.[73] He thus determined to launch himself into an independent business career. He was attracted by the idea of a liaison with Lister, whose interest in woolcombing technology was, in many ways, complementary to his own: 'As soon as I found that Mr. Lister was in possession of the patented main elements of the machine which I then had planned in embryo at least and which I regarded as the combing machine of the future,' he later recalled, 'I resolved to leave Cullingworth and put myself in the way of making his acquaintance and forming an alliance of some sort.'[74]

In 1846 Holden severed his links with Townends, established a worsted spinning business at Pit Lane, Bradford, and began to cultivate a connection with Lister. In spite of the forceful moral and monetary support of his wife, Marion, Holden encountered financial problems almost immediately.[75] Within months he was in debt to friends and banks, but conceded defeat before becoming bankrupt.[76] Meanwhile his relationship with Lister was developing on two fronts. As a worsted spinner, Holden required and received Lister's services as a producer of combed wool.[77] As an inventor, Holden's penury acted as a constraint upon his independent development, while Lister's wealth and his active interest in technological progress provided a potential solution.[78]

In 1847, Holden and Lister formed the association that was to become the most sustained and fruitful in terms of production and of technical development.[79] Important results were quickly yielded by their collaboration, demonstrating the wisdom of a partnership where drive and inventive ability were combined with business talent and financial acumen. The partners aimed to perfect the Square Motion machine, upon which Holden had been working for several years. Their improvements resulted in the first patent of the Square Motion comb, taken out in 1848 in Lister's name only, despite Holden's substantial input.[80] The perfection of the Square Motion which Holden claimed would become 'a most valuable one for merino wool',[81] encouraged the partners to consider means of extending their activities. The Square Motion machine was unusual among English designs in its ability to comb effectively the fine wools used in the French worsted industry, the significance of which Holden readily appreciated.[82] A further dimension was thus added to the relationship between Lister and Holden. Lister was anxious to maximise the gains from his monopoly of woolcombing patents and clearly harboured an extravagant desire to build factories across Europe.[83] His method of monopolising combing technology had not yet been emulated in France, except to a limited extent by Nicolas Schlumberger who owned Heilmann's patent: Lister was therefore poised to extend his quest for woolcombing monopoly across the Channel. Holden's ambitions were more restrained, but he too wished to become a successful businessman – and preferably distant from Bradford where he had once been thwarted.

Establishing a joint enterprise for combing wool in France would not only satisfy the objectives of both men but, more importantly, would make the most effective use of the machine on which they had cooperated. A partnership agreement was signed on 1 January 1849, after Holden had paid a visit to France to secure suitable factory premises.[84] In February of that year, the firm of Lister and Holden began operations in St Denis, a small town to the north of Paris.

The search for an effective and commercially viable machine to comb wool was, therefore, frustrating and protracted. On both sides of the Channel, many hopeful individuals invested considerable energy in finding a solution, yet few machines developed in the period 1790 to 1840 achieved practical success. Those most involved in solving the woolcombing problem were textile machine-makers who were undoubtedly drawn to it because of the challenge of the technical difficulties encountered. The early machines attracted little interest in the worsted industry, however, as both spinners and combers lacked enthusiasm for developing a woolcombing technology.[85]

During the 1840s, however, and particularly after 1845, the pace of invention quickened and Heilmann's patent of 1845/46, based as it was on entirely original precepts, marked the beginning of a new era in mechanical woolcombing technology. Several possible reasons exist for this surge of activity, the most plausible of which involved the renewed interest of the worsted spinners. Until the 1840s, the productivity gains of the factory spinners within the worsted industry maintained an upward path, the result of a combination of falling raw material prices and increased technical efficiency in spinning.[86]

Thereafter, in the spinning sector, productivity advances decelerated, encouraging worsted manufacturers to seek additional means of reducing the price of their yarn.[87] They turned their attention to traditionally organised preparatory stages, among which combing was the most important in terms of value added. Because of the expansion of the industry, it is also possible that a bottleneck had occurred in the labour-intensive combing sector.[88] Clearly, the spinners responded to the changed conditions by actively encouraging the development of a commercially viable woolcombing technology. It is no coincidence that the two individuals most financially committed to achieving such a goal – Samuel Cunliffe Lister and Nicolas Schlumberger – were both spinners.[89]

Despite the progress of the 1840s, it was several years before the worsted industry was transformed. The combing inventions of that decade were typically restricted, in the first instance, to use in the inventors' or the spinners' establishments where no competing techniques would be employed. This allowed the machine to be perfected in a factory environment, and fulfilled the right of the patentee to recoup some of the gains embodied in a superior technique. The commercial potential of the inventions of the 1840s was therefore not realised until the beginning of the next decade when the new machine combs first became available.

By 1850, woolcombing was on the point of profound transformation in France and England. Lister was in full command of the nature and direction of this change in England and he was intent upon achieving the same in France with his partner, Isaac Holden. The next chapter focuses on the precise manner in which this happened and on the outcome of the association of the two men.

Notes

1 Which also took many years to reach the stage of commercial viability.

2   D. J. Bird, 'The Holden Comb', B. Tech. dissertation, University of Bradford (Bradford, 1971), p. 8.
3   Elements of Cartwright's are apparent in the specifications of Noble's patent of 1853.
4   J. Burnley, The History of Wool and Woolcombing (London, 1889), p. 115.
5   A commercially-viable comb seemed possible from Collier's invention of 1828 but was most marked after 1840.
6   Burnley, Wool and Woolcombing, p. 144.
7   Ibid., p. 145.
8   J.-J. Hémardinquer, 'Une dynastie de mécaniciens anglais en France: James, John et Juliana Collier (1791–1847)', Revue d'histoire des sciences et de leurs applications, 17 (1964), pp. 194–200.
9   Ibid.
10 Ministère de l'Industrie et du Commerce, Brevets d'invention français 1791–1902, Un siècle de progrès technique (Paris, 1958), p. 92.
11 Hémardinquer, 'Une dynastie', loc. cit., p. 201; Burnley, Wool and Woolcombing, p. 151.
12 Bird, 'The Holden Comb', loc. cit., p. 9; Burnley, Wool and Woolcombing, p. 151.
13 Bird, loc. cit., p. 9.
14 For example, the industrial census of Paris in 1848 shows that the Collier comb accounted for two-thirds of all the machine combs used in the city's woolcombing industry (the remaining machines were of English origin): Statistique de l'industrie à Paris (Paris, 1851), p. 418.
15 Catalogue des Brevets d'invention, 1791–1827, 1828–1842, 1843–1844. France: Brevets d'invention sér. 1, 1791–1844.
16 For mechanical combing in England before the 1840s see: E. M. Sigsworth, Black Dyke Mills (Liverpool, 1958), p. 79; D.T. Jenkins and K.G. Ponting, The British Wool Textile Industry, 1770–1914 (London, 1982), pp. 106–9; J. James, The History and Topography of Bradford (London, 1841), p. 279; J. M. Trickett, 'A Technological Appraisal of the Isaac Holden Papers', M. Sc. dissertation, University of Bradford (Bradford, 1977), p. 13.
17 In 1834 and 1836, Noble introduced a continuous feeding mechanism; in 1835, Donisthorpe patented sliding teeth.
18 This account of Holden's early life is based upon more detailed versions in HIL, pp. 1–23, 767–78; E. M. Sigsworth 'Sir Isaac Holden, Bt.: the First Comber in Europe', in N. B. Harte and K. G. Ponting (eds), Textile History and Economic History (Manchester, 1973), pp. 340–2; and Trickett, 'A Technological Appraisal', pp. 21–8. The most recent biography is E. Jennings, 'Sir Isaac Holden (1807–1897): "The First Comber in Europe"', Ph. D. thesis (University of Bradford, 1982).
19 An early episode reflecting Holden's inventiveness concerns the discovery of the match during his stay in Leeds. See Trickett, 'A Technological Appraisal', pp. 26–8.
20 B-77.
21 Letter to Rev. G. Marsland, 29 October 1838 in HIL, pp. 72–6.
22 B-77, and 'Retrospective Notes' in his memorandum book, B-91/3: 'Wool was carded and combed on Collier's machine to our knowledge as far back as 1834. The system Collier was known and practised in Paris during the exhibition of 1834 when I saw it at work on Collier's premises.'
23 B-77. Subsequent behaviour suggests that Holden was reluctant to patent any of his ideas until they were perfect.
24 Burnley, Wool and Woolcombing, pp. 155–6.
25 Bird, 'The Holden Comb', pp. 9–10.
26 Burnley, Wool and Woolcombing, p. 156.

27 Bird, 'The Holden Comb', p. 11.
28 *Ibid.*, p. 12.
29 *Ibid.*, p. 13. Before they met, Lister and Holden had been interested in similar technical problems, though Holden had developed the Square Motion in essentials before they joined forces. The Square Motion was so-called because the combs were operated by quadrangular frames. See Bird, 'The Holden Comb', p. 18.
30 Donisthorpe went into production temporarily with others in France in direct competition to Lister and Holden in the mid-1850s'.
31 The cost difference was not great as handcombers demanded relatively high wages.
32 A close examination of Holden's experiments and trials with the Collier comb is provided in Trickett, 'A Technological Appraisal', pp. 56–71.
33 The 'Nip' was probably the first commercially viable machine comb used in England.
34 *Statistique de l'industrie à Paris* (Paris, 1851), p. 418.
35 *Bulletin de la Société Industrielle de Mulhouse* (hereafter *BSIM*) vol. 21, 104 (1848), p. 256. This was the chief worsted mill in Alsace, accounting for 43 per cent of the region's total spindlage. The firm subsequently changed its name twice, first to Risler, Schwartz et Cie, and then to Schwartz, Trapp et Cie. See M. Lévy-Leboyer, *Les Banques européennes et l'industrialisation internationale dans la première moitié du XIXe siècle* (Paris, 1964), p. 163.
36 *Exposition des produits de l'industrie française en 1839: Rapport du Jury Central* (Paris, 1839), vol. 1, p. 37. At the same exhibition, Juliana Collier was awarded a gold medal (*Ibid.*, vol. 2, pp 30–1).
37 A. Falleur, *L'industrie lainière dans la région de Fourmies* (Paris, 1930), p. 26; *Le Nord Industriel* (June 1966), special supplement, 'Les Pionniers', p. 71.
38 *Ibid.*
39 The figure for Paris is taken from *Statistique de l'industrie à Paris*, p. 418. The actual number given is 84, but of these, 25 were not true combs but resembled more carding machines. *Exposition Universelle de 1851: Travaux de la commission française* (Paris, 1854), vol. 4, p. 143. The figures for the Nord and Reims are taken from *Statistique de la France* (Paris, 1847), vol. 1, pp. 83, 175. All the combs in the Nord seem to have been concentrated in the Fourmies-Le Cateau region. See E. Lefévre, *Histoire économique de la laine* (Reims, 1906), p. 290.
40 *Ibid.*
41 B-91/6.
42 French patents from *Subject Matter Index: Patents for Inventions Granted in France from 1791 to 1876 inclusive* (Washington, 1883), pp. 196–9, 925–30; British patents from Burnley, *Wool and Woolcombing*, pp. 423–9.
43 These machines are described in Burnley, *Wool and Woolcombing*, pp. 428–9. An excellent discussion of combing history is to be found in Trickett, 'A Technological Appraisal', pp. 48–105. Three undergraduate theses have been produced at the University of Bradford on the most influential machine combs: D. J. Bird, 'The Holden Comb' (1971); M. H. Walker, 'The Lister Comb' (1973); and W. J. Machin 'The Noble Comb' (1974).
44 *Subject Matter Index*, p. 197; W. O. Henderson, *Britain and Industrial Europe, 1750–1870* (Leicester, 1972), p. 81; C. Fohlen, *L'industrie textile au temps du second empire* (Paris, 1956), p.103; A. Goblet, *Le peignage de la laine à Roubaix-Tourcoing et son évolution économique et sociale* (Lille, 1903), p. 63.
45 It may have been influenced by Girard's flax-hackling machine. See Trickett, 'A Technological Appraisal', p. 77.

46   *BSIM*, vol. 21, 104, pp. 443–4.

47   *Ibid.*, pp. 445, 449–50.

48   Heilmann failed in his own business and may have become highly inventive as a result.

49   *Ibid.*, p. 440.

50   *Ibid.*, pp. 272–3.

51   Burnley, *Wool and Woolcombing*, p. 241.

52   Schlumberger did however incur considerable expense in efforts to preserve the originality of Heilmann's machine and prevent imitations. See Chapter 3, pp. 28–9.

53   In 1848, for example, it was satisfactorily adapted for wool. See Henderson, *Britain and Industrial Europe*, p. 81.

54   Burnley, *Wool and Woolcombing*, p. 219.

55   It was believed to have been inspired by his wife and daughters combing their long hair. Their gentle action on the end, with spreaded fingers separating the strands, removed knots without damaging the hair. This action Heilmann attempted to replicate.

56   M. Alcan, *Fabrication des étoffes: Traité du travail des laines peignées* (Paris, 1873), p. 197.

57   *Ibid.*, pp. 212–13.

58   *Ibid.*, p. 213.

59   *Ibid.*

60   *Ibid.*, p. 214.

61   Burnley, *Wool and Woolcombing*, pp. 251, 259: though, in fact, the 'Nip' differed from the Heilmann comb in several important respects; for example, the 'Nip' drew the wool through the teeth in a horizontal motion, while the Heilmann machine combed the wool through the teeth in a circular pattern. See *ibid.*, p. 251.

62   *Ibid.*, p. 222.

63   *Ibid.*

64   *Ibid.*, p. 240. He therefore more than recouped the expense of buying the patent through the increased sales of his own machine.

65   It was used in the Lancashire cotton industry. See *ibid.*, p. 240.

66   *Ibid.*

67   D.T. Jenkins and K.G. Ponting. *The British Wool Textile Industry, 1770–1914* (London, 1982), p. 109.

68   This seems to be more the case in England than in France, though in both countries the productivity gains of the spinners were failing to maintain growth.

69   Burnley, *Wool and Woolcombing*, p. 429.

70   *Ibid*, p. 261.

71   Sigsworth, *Black Dyke Mills*, pp. 39–40.

72   The exact date of their first meeting is uncertain.

73   *HIL*, p. 130; B-91.

74   B-77.

75   B-91.

76   B-58. 'Rest assured,' he wrote to his banker Laycock in Bradford in 1848, 'I shall give up my business before I lose it all.' Six months later, however, he was able to write a very different letter: 'We have paid every farthing of our projected outlay here, say £120000...the profits will enable me...to withdraw sums of £1000 per month...what interest can you give me?' (L-VII/7).

77   He was reluctant to call upon Lister's help in this way, but: 'I have no chance except to get wool combed by him' (2 October 1846; B-91).

78   Though he resented being beholden to Lister and had hoped to be an equal partner.

79 Within ten years, they owned and were responsible for the bulk of woolcombing inventions and Holden became the largest woolcomber in Europe. See Chapters 4–7, below *passim*.
80 This was the cause of much acrimony for many years after the end of the partnership. Both men claimed to be the real inventor of the Square Motion. See Epilogue, this volume.
81 B-91.
82 It could also be argued that Holden had a move in mind while inventing a machine specifically intended for French conditions.
83 He already had several mills in England and one in Germany. See Sigsworth, *Black Dyke Mills*, p. 40 n.
84 L-I. Earlier versions of the partnership were drawn up on 25 October and 1 November 1848 (13–58).
85 Some adventurous French manufacturers did, however, experiment with the Collier comb, for example in Paris and Alsace.
86 French worsted spinners preferred to use the mule (in contrast to their British counterparts who had abandoned it in favour of throstle and cap frame spinning methods). Though the self-acting type diffused slowly (in 1850 it accounted for only 5 per cent of worsted spindlage), productivity advances on the manually-operated mule were impressive. Successive improvement of the mule, leading to greater speeds and reliability, resulted in increasing yarn fineness and economies of scale – between 1825 and 1851, spinners more than quadrupled the fineness of their weft and nearly doubled the spinning capacity of the mule. The economic implications were considerable. Yarn prices between 1822 and 1850 fell from 65 francs per kg to 14 francs per kg; and the commission spinning price (directly reflecting physical productivity) in Fourmies between 1825 and 1850 fell from 140 francs for 1000 lengths to 30 francs for an equivalent amount. Similar economies were achieved in the fixed and running costs of the average worsted mill. See *Exposition Universelle de 1851*, pp. 148, 151–2, 156; Falleur, *L'industrie lainière*, p. 44; J. H. Clapham, *The Woollen and Worsted Industries* (London, 1907), p. 55; Jenkins and Ponting, *British Wool Textile Industry*, pp. 264–5 which also contains equivalent information on British worsted spinning.
87 C. Marteau, *Tableau synoptique de l'industrie lainière, 1789–1900* (Reims, 1900); T. J. Markovitch, 'L'industrie française de 1789 à 1964', *Cahiers de l'ISÉA*, ser. AF, 6 (1966), Tables 6 and 16: Falleur, *L'industrie lainière*, pp. 38–9, 44, 72. Sigsworth, *Black Dyke Mills*, pp. 32–4, 200–1.
88 It can be estimated that the demand for handcombers in the period 1844 to 1847 was 70 per cent greater than in the period 1829–44 (calculated from *Statistique de la France: industrie 1861–65* (Nancy, 1873) p. XLIX; *ADM*, 172–3 and *Exposition Universelle* (1851), vol. IV, p. 155.
89 Other prominent individuals in employing machine combs of their own designs were Paturle-Lupin of Le Cateau, and Seillière of Alsace.

3 Patents and Technological Control: the Lister–Holden Partnership, 1848–60

This chapter examines the partnership between Samuel Cunliffe Lister and Isaac Holden with emphasis on the means by which their common interest in mechanical woolcombing was used to fulfil their capitalist ambitions. The focus, therefore, is upon the competition for technological leadership and the interaction of Lister and Holden's business concerns with their fight for patent control. Astute manipulation of the relatively new patent system was the means by which Lister and Holden not only became rich and successful, but also influenced the nature of the diffusion of woolcombing technology in both France and Britain.

The operation of an effective national patent system became necessary as technical developments proliferated, especially in France and Britain from the late eighteenth century onwards. Several crucial inventions were unprotected in any formal sense, and their inventors unrewarded. Discretionary grants were made to such contributors to industrial technology as Cartwright and Crompton, but only after pressure was brought to bear on government by grateful capitalists.[1]

Patent laws had existed for many years in both France and Britain, but not until the early nineteenth century was the system modified to offer reasonable protection and recompense to an inventor. The aim of this revision was to acquire for the patentee some control over the use of his invention; in other words, to grant the inventor an effective monopoly.[2] By thus allowing the patentee to determine the extent of the use of his invention and thereby creating a scarcity, the inventor was able to secure an economic rent. The size of the reward to the inventor can be interpreted as a measurement of the invention's usefulness to society, but also as a reflection of the patentee's skill at exploiting the system.[3]

Despite apparent abuses of the patent laws, the existence of such legislation was crucial for the emergence of specialised industrial technology in the nineteenth century. Because of the secretive nature of invention, particularly in the context of intense competition, patent laws were necessary to stimulate the conception and disclosure of new ideas and their subsequent exploitation by the capitalist.[4]

Clearly, the extent and direction of invention in woolcombing technology during the first half of the nineteenth century was encouraged by the introduction of effective patent laws on both sides of the Channel. In the important French law of 1791, protection was guaranteed to the author of a discovery for an optional period of five, ten or fifteen years.[5] To facilitate the rapid diffusion of industrial technology, an Imperial Decree of 1810 granted to the importer to France of any foreign discovery the same rights as to the inventor for the period remaining on the patent in the country of origin.[6]

In 1844, patent legislation allowed French nationals for the first time to patent their inventions abroad, and foreign inventors were given the right to take out a French patent. Patents of importation were thus discontinued.[7] When the surge in mechanical woolcombing developments took place in the 1840s, therefore, an effectively reciprocal patent system had emerged between Britain and France, and most of the important inventions were protected by both a French and a British patent.[8]

While the patent system clearly enhanced the output of woolcombing inventions from the 1840s onwards, it also permitted the introduction of entirely novel business practices which directly influenced the nature of the industry's organisation. It was Samuel Cunliffe Lister who had initiated the technique of purchasing patents on inventions in competition with his own designs in order to secure a monopoly of woolcombing technology. At first, this activity was confined to British patents, but in 1848 he determined to extend his field of purchase to France where his system had few competitors.[9] In obtaining a technological monopoly, or near monopoly, Lister was in a position to influence the diffusion of woolcombing machines and thus to exert some control over the nature of production.[10] In England, he was able to limit the use of machine combs to his own, and in France he hoped to contain the spread of competing machines.[11]

Lister and Holden's articulated aims in purchasing patents were consistent with the specific objectives of patent consolidation. F. L. Vaughan, an authority on patents, specifies these objectives: to create a monopoly of an industry by controlling alternative inventions and their improvements; to avoid the scrapping of existing equipment; to combine into a superior product or process the best ideas of various inventions; and to avoid litigation.[12]

Lister's strategy was closest to the first of these. His ultimate aim in accumulating all relevant patents was to remove competition by controlling woolcombing technology in both England and France.[13] Holden's aim initially was closest to the third objective. He hoped to perfect the Square Motion machine comb and to deal with potential competitors by producing the finest combed wool.[14]

Throughout the years of their partnership, both men stuck rigidly to their own strategies. Though theoretically complementary, the strategies began to drive the men apart, leading eventually to the collapse of their partnership after ten years.[15] For the most part, however, the objectives of their association were satisfied, though Holden gained the most from it.

The year in which Lister and Holden began to produce combed wool in St Denis, 1849, marked the onset of a critical decade for French woolcombing and for the partners' own fortunes. The ten-year partnership was characterised by frenetic patent activity, and in woolcombing generally, by the growth of competition and the fight for leadership.[16] There seems little doubt, however, that the presence of Lister and Holden in France influenced the nature and pace of change throughout the country.

From the outset, the partners were determined to maintain their interest in and control over the developing technology as an essential adjunct to their manufacturing activity. They had become associated through a common curiosity in mechanical woolcombing, but their perceptions on how this interest might best be exploited differed. In particular, they consistently failed to agree on two vital issues: the question of which techniques at their disposal should be employed in production; and the nature and extent of patent purchases.[17]

Holden's paramount concern was to perfect the Square Motion machine comb, in which he had great faith, and to maximise its commercialisation.[18] He believed that his machine would achieve great success in France because of the apparent ease with which it combed the fine merino wool on which the French worsted industry was based.[19] Holden thus assumed that the Square Motion alone, once operational, would be adopted at St Denis.[20] Lister, however, had a low opinion of the Square Motion. He felt that it had 'nothing to it',[21] while his own machine, the 'Nip', was the 'best in the world'.[22] Lister was determined that the 'Nip' should not only be used at St Denis, but should also be diffused more widely in France.[23] While it is likely that the 'Nip' was ready for commercial application before the Square Motion, early trials as St Denis suggested that it was much less suited to merino wool. The 'Nip' was brought temporarily into use at St Denis when the Square Motion experienced teething troubles, but its operation was so unsatisfactory that Holden's machine was rapidly re-introduced.[24] Holden continued to improve the Square Motion until it was operationally supreme, while Lister was more concerned with accumulating patents of competing machines than in perfecting his own woolcombing technology.[25] The fulfilment of Lister's goal proved to be expensive and time-consuming.[26] Although he was willing and able to expend enormous sums, the selection of the most appropriate patents for purchase was extraordinarily difficult. Between 1845 and 1855, there was a rush of discoveries, and textile patents in both France and Britain were dominated by designs for woolcombing machines.[27] It was no easy task to abstract from the mass the most commercially valuable ideas, yet it was crucial to act decisively during the 1850s if control of woolcombing production were to be achieved.[28]

The inventive activity of the 1840s and 1850s is indicated in the number of woolcombing patents (see Table 3.1).

Table 3.1: Patents granted for wool machine combs, 1840–54

	France	England
1840–44	11	9
1845–49	2	12
1850–54	9	66
1855–59	13	48

Sources: France – *Subject Matter Index*, pp. 196–9, 925–30.
England – Burnley, *Wool and Woolcombing*, pp. 426–41.

In Britain, techniques proliferated in the 1850s and 1860s; in France, activity had also been high during the mid-1840s. As the typical length of a French patent was fifteen years, many patents were due to expire in or about 1860. Table 3.2 indicates that this was true of several important French patents, most notably that of Heilmann (subsequently owned by Schlumberger), whose machine comb was rapidly adopted in the major worsted producing regions in France.[29] In order to realise the greatest gains of patent purchasing in France, therefore, and to recoup the cost involved, action had to be swift.[30]

Table 3.2: Predominant French woolcombing patents

Name of patentee	Date taken out	Length of patent	Date of expiry
1. Paturle-Lupin/ Seydoux Sieber	22 April 1845	5 years	1850
2. Bernier-Thibout	15 November 1845	15 years	1860
3. Seillière & Heywood	8 December 1845	15 years	1860
4. J. Heilmann	17 December 1845	15 years	1860
5. Hubner	27 August 1851	15 years	1866
6. Dujardin–Collette	24 September 1851	15 years	1866
7. N. Schlumberger	23 September 1852	15 years	1867
8. Noble	7 May 1853	(14 years on English patent taken out 1852)	1866

Source: Catalogue des Brevets d'Invention (1844–46), (1852–53).

The problems associated with Lister's course of action were compounded by the frequency of expensive litigation. Legal hearings were quite common during periods of concentrated or prolific developments in technology, to distinguish infringements of patents from genuine improvements. Lister's actions, therefore, would inevitably lead to involvement in legal wrangles, but he remained undeterred. He possessed sufficient instinct and determination to surmount the many difficulties and to succeed in his quest.[31]

The first problem was encountered soon after Holden's arrival in St Denis. Paturle-Lupin and Seydoux, the giant worsted manufacturers of Le Cateau, claimed that the Square Motion infringed their patents of 1845 and 1846.[32] Although this was quickly resolved, the partnership was soon in dispute again, this time with Seillière, whose patent, taken out with Heywood, both of Alsace, in 1844, contained much of interest to Holden.[33] Lister, having returned to England to tend his enterprises there, advised Holden, who was in sole charge at St Denis.[34] Lister's response to the Seillière problem illustrates his talent as a tactician:

> The best plan...would be to allow him to obtain a verdict against you, upon condition that you and he should jointly use the patent, and if necessary that you should jointly support it, but that no licence should be granted to anyone else to use it. You would then both benefit by the protection of the patent and it upset neither of you.[35]

Such a deal suited both parties and it was formulated early in 1851.

The early success of the St Denis enterprise led, early in 1851, to the consideration of the purchase of an additional factory site. This was to be in the north of France, by this time the centre of the French worsted industry.[36] Lister was determined to adopt the 'Nip' machine there and to spread its use more widely in France, while preventing Schlumberger from supplying the trade with more Heilmann machines.[37]

In 1852, however, Lister experienced his first encounter with Schlumberger, who believed that the 'Nip' infringed the Heilmann patent.[38] The implications of this dispute were far-reaching. The Heilmann comb was the closest rival of both the Square Motion and the 'Nip', and by the time of the clash between the two men, was already in great demand in France.[39] Schlumberger had been aware of the 'Nip' since its patent of 1850/51, but had not challenged it in the courts as an infringement of the Heilmann patent until its commercial use was imminent. The infringement trial was heard in February/March 1852, and it found in Schlumberger's favour.[40] Undeterred, Lister obtained the rights to sell the Heilmann comb in England, which effectively prevented its sale there.[41] By 1853, therefore, Lister controlled all the important English woolcombing patents and produced only his own 'Nip' machine for distribution in England.[42] By this means, he made large profits on his

English activities, quickly recouping the outlay on the Heilmann patent. The dispute with Schlumberger was the first of many that resulted in litigation. In the following years, several law suits and patent purchases became necessary to defend the 'Nip' both in England and France.[43] In addition, Lister continued in his attempt to control the Heilmann comb in France by purchasing the French patent from Schlumberger.[44]

By 1852/53, the partners' activities – both those for which they were jointly responsible, and those in which they engaged independently – had become diverse and complex.[45] Two new factories had been opened (at Reims and Croix) and success was consistently achieved. While the methods of Lister and Holden seemed fundamentally at variance, and were the cause of much bitter dispute, they were, by chance, complementary. Although it is impossible to quantify the long-term value of Lister's capital-intensive activity, it clearly influenced the degree of success achieved by Holden and his Square Motion.[46]

Because Lister and Holden's patenting activities coincided with the peak output of mechanical woolcombing devices, litigation was a feature of their partnership for its duration. After the major encounter with Schlumberger, several further setbacks occurred in Lister's quest to gain effective control over French woolcombing technology.[47] In 1853, Preller, Eastwood and Gamble patented an improved machine comb in competition with the 'Nip', and probably the Heilmann comb. A private judgment in the following year found the machine to be an infringement of the Donisthorpe and Lister patents.[48]

A more lasting dispute surrounded the 1855 patent taken out by Samuel Crabtree for an improved machine comb. The machine was believed to infringe in principle or detail the inventions of Heilmann, Donisthorpe, Lister and Preller.[49] The first defence of the 'Nip' against the Crabtree machine was heard in 1856. This 'most costly trial' – the so-called 'Lister's Leather' after the alleged infringer of the 'Nip' patent – found in Lister's favour. Leather appealed against the judgment but it was upheld in the Court of Appeal.[50] By the autumn of 1856, therefore, the validity of Lister's patents and their infringement by Crabtree's machine had been clearly established.

In France, however, Lister's battle against the Crabtree machine persisted to the late 1850s. In 1858, Duriez fils, users of the Crabtree machine, were taken to court by Lister.[51] To simplify proceedings, the case centred on the Crabtree machine as an infringement of the Preller patent only, which Lister had acquired upon the decision that it infringed the 'Nip'.[52] The Crabtree machine was clearly a copy of Preller in several important respects, particularly in the design and combination of instruments, and the hearing agreed that the imitation was evident.[53] Lister subsequently became reluctant to pursue the question of infringement with firms working Crabtree's machine for fear of reducing the value of his French interest. Further suits, he believed, 'would damage the sale of the concern more than £50,000'.[54]

It was, however, Lister's former colleague, Donisthorpe, who posed the greatest threat to the partners' progress. Donisthorpe, who, in the late 1840s, had temporarily cooperated with Noble, was responsible for improvements to the Noble comb in 1853, and subsequently acquired the Noble patent.[55] By 1855, it seemed that Donisthorpe was preparing to produce combed wool in France, using a further modified Noble comb, probably the closest rival of both the 'Nip' and the Square Motion.[56]

Lister, clearly troubled by this prospect sought means to reduce its potential effect. He proceeded on the assumption that the Noble comb was an infringement of the Heilmann comb, and renewed his efforts to purchase the latter.[57] If successful, he would automatically gain control of the Noble comb. Lister, however, had an additional anxiety, which obscured the optimal course of action. He was aware that Donisthorpe might sell his patent to Schlumberger, once the Noble comb was ready for commercial use and if it were shown to be an infringement.[58] Lister's fear was that if Donisthorpe did follow this course of action, Schlumberger would strengthen his position over Lister as holder of woolcombing patents: 'I insist upon the purchase of Noble, because in Schlumberger's hands it would do us much mischief.'[59] To pre-empt such a move,therefore, Lister offered Donisthorpe 50 per cent of his share in the St Denis concern. Donisthorpe declined, ostensibly because of his uncertainty over the viability of the business, and the problem of competing patents remained.[60]

During 1855, Lister's financial problems compounded the difficulties of assuming control of French woolcombing patents to the extent that he contemplated selling out. 'I have decided to sell my share in the French concern,' he wrote to Holden

> although we are doing well now in six months' time we shall have little or no profit if we allow a rival concern to grow. . . .I shall sell my share. . .and £20,000 to include all my patents so far as they apply to woolcombing for France and I will engage not to be mixed up in any rival concern for woolcombing.[61]

Lister's fear of Donisthorpe's competition was reflected in his second suggestion – that of buying out Holden before joining forces with Donisthorpe: 'I have no wish to run any risk of rival concerns.'[62]

His financial problems apparently abated, however, for he followed neither course, and eventually decided to renew his commitment to Holden and their French concerns, and to continue to consolidate a portfolio of competing woolcombing patents. In a characteristic letter to Holden, Lister remarked: 'If I continue to keep any share in the business, I should certainly advise the purchase of [the Noble patent] also of Schlumberger and Preller and then you may bid defiance to everybody and make an enormous profit.'[63] This final stage of consolidation, Lister believed, could be achieved at the cost of £30,000.[64]

By 1856, the Noble comb was ready for commercial use, following the introduction of a particular feed apparatus by the newly-formed syndicate of Tavernier, Crofts and Donisthorpe, who then prepared to launch the machine onto the French market and into production.[65] In July 1856, the firm of Tavernier, Crofts and Donisthorpe bought a mill near Paris, and in September opened their Paris office.[66] Because Lister believed the improved Noble comb to have usurped the 'Nip's' position as the 'best in the world'[67], his real fear was that Tavernier and company would damage Lister and Holden's position by selling the Noble comb and undercutting the process:

> I do not so much fear competition in combing as I do in selling machines as they cannot for a length of time oppose us on a large scale, but even on a small scale they may and will damage our process – in my opinion they will sell a large number of machines as there is no doubt that for many sorts of wool it is a first-rate machine. So long as we had the best machine we were masters but I doubt it now.[68]

Lister's response to this threat to his monopoly highlights the complexity of patent consolidation, the delicate interaction of the competitors, as well as Lister's unusual ability to devise possible solutions. Lister's immediate reaction was to attempt to purchase the patent for the Noble comb in France; but because his ultimate objective was to buy out Schlumberger's entire French woolcombing interests, he conceived a more subtle plan.[69] He instructed his lawyer to investigate the possibility that the Noble patent infringed Hubner's patent, also from the Schlumberger stable.

> My chief object in the purchase of Noble was to protect France, but if the patent is doubtful, of course I must decline having anything to do with it until the point is cleared up to the satisfaction of my lawyers. Can you buy Hubner for France? If so, we need not care a farthing for Noble.[70]

Before this was determined, however, Lister formulated an alternative and more ambitious strategy: to reach an agreement with Schlumberger for the purchase of both the Heilmann and the Hubner patents together with unspecified others. This would have the dual effect of safeguarding the standing of Lister and Holden as combers, while keeping the Noble comb at bay, and forcing Donisthorpe to part with it if it proved to be an infringement of the Hubner patent.[71] The scheme, however, failed to take account of the possibility that the Noble comb did not infringe Hubner; and because Lister was growing increasingly anxious about a potential agreement between Tavernier, Crofts and Donisthorpe, and Schlumberger for the latter to manufacture the Noble comb, he devised an all-embracing scheme: 'Now I have a rough programme of a plan which for a trifling sum will give you the undisturbed monopoly of France for years to come.'[72]

Under the terms of this strategy, Donisthorpe was to be displaced by the tempting offer of £20,000 for the Noble patent. Schlumberger, the more resistant and expensive obstacle, would be induced to part with his woolcombing interest by a substantial financial reward, including a generous lump-sum for his collection of patents and a *pro rata* payment for each of the machines subsequently sold. By this means Schlumberger's share of the market would be reduced and the way would be cleared for the introduction of Lister's 'Nip' in France.[73]

The plan was rapidly put into motion, with Holden conducting the initial negotiations. In August 1856, Holden held apparently fruitful discussions with Schlumberger.[74] Two months later, Lister and Schlumberger reached an agreement, transferring to Lister and Holden for £15,000 the right to Schlumberger's patents, the exclusive licence for the Noble comb and the power to stop it from being worked or sold in France, except to the extent that he, Lister, desired it.[75] Because the formalisation of this agreement was delayed,[76] Lister activated a contingency plan. He initiated negotiations with Donisthorpe with the aim of achieving similar results. The proposals that emerged from these discussions were first, that the rights to the Noble comb would be transferred to Lister and Holden who would share with Donisthorpe the profits on its sale; and secondly, that the expense of purchasing Schlumberger's woolcombing patents would be borne among the three men.[77]

Another year passed before an arrangement satisfactory to all interested parties was formalised. In the meantime, the implications of the existence of a large number of competing and overlapping patents and a smaller number of often conflicting interacting personalities, became apparent. Several powerful individuals, both inventors and producers, aware of Lister's intention to buy them out, made stringent efforts to resist this. Indeed, a consortium was envisaged that intended to jeopardise the monopoly, even the success, of Holden. John Crofts (of Tavernier, Crofts and Donisthorpe) proposed a giant concern that would embrace all the competing groups.[78] This combine would control all the relevant patents and would manufacture the Noble comb.[79] Lister, by this time jaded by his difficult French experience, considered supporting – even joining – this venture as a means of off-loading the burden of anxiety and expenditure, while only partially compromising the fulfilment of his goal.[80] Holden was less attracted by the idea, and was quick to propose an alternative means of sharing the gains. He suggested an assembly of all interested firms, machinery and patent-holders into an enormous and impracticable limited liability company.[81]

Happily for the future of the French enterprises, these bizarre schemes were rendered superfluous by a momentous agreement between Lister and Holden, and Schlumberger signed on 19 June 1857.[82] By it, Schlumberger sold to Lister and Holden his entire stock of woolcombing patents for £35,000 (of which the most important were those of Heilmann and Hubner), but continued to construct Heilmann machine combs under licence. Similar arrangements were made for the Noble machine comb constructed in Louviers by Mercier, a prominent textile machine-maker.[83] The Square Motion machine comb remained the sole property of Lister and Holden.

Lister had long hoped for an agreement with Schlumberger, but it is doubtful whether this agreement fully met his objectives. It did not directly suppress the Heilmann machine comb; nor would the likely revenue from licence fees cover the costs incurred.[84] Indeed, Lister's ultimate goal was only partially achieved. He had gained a monopoly of French woolcombing patents (admittedly for not as long as he wished), but his own machine, the 'Nip', was never used in France, except experimentally.[85] The protection of the Square Motion machine comb featured little in Lister's overall scheme. His generally low opinion of the machine, despite its manifest success, persisted throughout the partnership and reflected, in Holden's opinion at least, Lister's lack of confidence in the management of the French business.[86]

Lister's patent purchases and the litigation frequently arising from them required continual funding. Of the many enterprises under his control, those in France produced the best and most regular profits and it was to them that Lister constantly turned for finance.[87] Holden deeply resented this imposition as he wished to use the profits of the business to build up the capital stock and to improve the performance of the Square Motion machine comb. His reactions to Lister's demands for cash were usually evasive, often contrary, and caused much bitterness between the two men.

In 1857, Lister's financial problems came to a head as the expensive agreement with Schlumberger coincided with the failure (or near failure) of several of his English concerns in the wake of the financial crisis of that year.[88] Holden turned this combination of events to his advantage as their relationship became increasingly strained. Rather than advancing cash, Holden, by then in a position of strength, offered to buy out Lister as he became desperate for cash.[89] After several attempts, Lister finally succumbed, and in December 1858 he agreed to sell his entire interest in the French business to Holden for £74,000, leaving Holden in overall control.[90]

Whereas the agreement with Schlumberger ironically signalled Lister's permanent departure from France, it was a major *coup* for Holden, and coincided perfectly with his relatively modest aims. The agreement not only protected Holden's cherished technique but, equally important, by owning the Heilmann patent, it allowed Holden to incorporate the best features of the rival machine comb into his own.[91]

Holden did ultimately appreciate the value of seeking and purchasing competing patents, however, and was occasionally involved in litigation on his own account as well as on Lister's behalf. The expense and aggravation involved was more than returned by the high-quality machine he consequently developed, and kept to himself. In his concern to conceal his machine from competitors, however, Holden followed two strategies: the Square Motion was constructed in Bradford, (or assembled in France from parts manufactured in Bradford and English firms in Lille); and, he failed to specify fully its components when patenting improvements.[92] On more than one occasion, Holden was forced to take legal action against imitators of the Square Motion. The most celebrated case was that against Vigoureux, leading woollen and worsted spinners in Reims. The hearing took place early in 1858, when it was disclosed that the confidential improvements to the Square Motion being tried out in anticipation of patenting, were stolen from Holden's works by J. Kendall, acting under instruction from Vigoureux.[93] Vigoureux then had Square Motion-type machines made up and adopted in his combing works. The arrangement and details of Vigoureux's machine were identical to Holden's, though it was generally believed to be an inferior copy. The court accepted Holden's arguments that his improvements pre-dated Vigoureux's and the latter was found to be in contravention of Holden's 1853 patent.[94]

Although the relationship between Lister and Holden was uneasy, the partnership had lasting significance for French woolcombing.[95] The response of the two men to manipulation of the patent system reflected their fundamentally different aims and aspirations. Despite frequent disagreements, the partners essentially operated independently, each fulfilling his own goal until their differences created operational incompatibility.

For Holden at least, it was a successful means to an end.[96] Lister's pursuit of patent consolidation had managed to reduce a plethora of competing and complementary patents to three machine combs, each with particular conditions attached to their use. It also taught Holden an invaluable lesson for his fortunes as a French woolcomber. The

Square Motion machine comb was fully protected and Holden set his mind on the manufacturing side of the business and on the problems of conducting business in a foreign country.

Notes

1 Petitions, indicating the extent of the use of a machine, were presented to the government who made an *ex gratia* payment reflecting the value of the machine.
2 E. T. Penrose, *The Economics of the International Patent System* (Baltimore, 1951), p. 1.
3 *Ibid.*, p. 28. The reward was not necessarily a reflection of the worth of the machine. Lister, for example, was able to earn enormous amounts from his own and others' patents.
4 *Ibid.*, pp. 31–2.
5 B. M. Rimmer, *Guide to Industrial Property Literature: France* (London 1980), pp. 1–2.
6 *Ibid.*
7 *Ibid.*
8 By the mid-1840s, all restrictions on the export of machinery from Britain had been lifted.
9 Nicolas Schlumberger was the chief competitor; he owned the Heilmann and Hubner patents.
10 The influence which this practice had on the movement towards woolcombing as a specialist activity is fully discussed in Chapter 5.
11 He was clearly too late to stop the spread of the Heilmann machine comb. See Chapter 7, pp. 79–80.
12 F. L. Vaughan, *The United States Patent System* (Norman, Okla., 1956), p. 69.
13 E.M. Sigsworth, *Black Dyke Mills* (Liverpool, 1958), p. 40 n.
14 *Enquête industrielle sur le traité de commerce avec l'Angleterre* (Paris, 1860), vol. 3, pp. 479–89; Isaac Holden to Samuel Lister 23 April 1855 (B-62).
15 The partnership was threatened with dissolution regularly. The first occasion was only weeks after its establishment (B-59).
16 Holden articulated these anxieties when he wrote retrospectively (1860) of the period: 'I and my late partner have taken many patents...and have bought many in order not to be [hindered] in improving our machinery. Combing is yet an infant industry requiring successive inventions and the reason why we take so many patents yet imperfect, is because we cannot safely begin to construct a new machine or apply an improvement till we have protected it by a patent' (B-65).
17 The most important choice was between the 'Nip' and the Square Motion machine comb. Lister and Holden also argued about whether to sell these machines and how to organise woolcombing production.
18 This had been the case since his early years at Cullingworth and continued to be so. His confidence was well rewarded.
19 In his desire to get away from Bradford, however, he had enquired about the state of the worsted industry and woolcombing in particular, in both France and the United States. The responses suggested to him that France would be a better bet. See *HIL*, pp. 127–32; and L-VI/8, 9, 10.
20 The machine experienced teething trouble and required modifications before it could be brought into full-time use at St Denis.
21 Samuel Lister to Isaac Holden, 8 January 1851 (B-60).
22 Samuel Lister to Isaac Holden, 24 May 1851 (B-60). He admonished Holden frequently for wasting time on perfecting the Square Motion, but

was nevertheless anxious that no one else should get hold of the system: 'I think you are not acting wisely in sending wool to Thuillier to card. I would rather forgo a little profit than call his attention and that of the trade to your system (Samuel Lister to Isaac Holden, 12 November 1851; B-60).

23   Samuel Lister to Isaac Holden, 2 January 1851 and 8 November 1851 (B-60).

24   Though Lister refused to give up the 'Nip' and claimed that by selling it they would be able to clear more than £50,000. Holden retorted that it was the Square Motion that had saved the St Denis concern (23 January 1851; B-60).

25   He nevertheless remained obsessional about keeping his work secret.

26   The main reason was the expansion of patents and the incidence of infringements. Lister's vigilance had to be constant. The issues were complex – his activities required not only technical expertise, but also knowledge of both French and English legal procedures. Lister and Holden employed the services of two leading patent agents in London – Carpmael and Brookes – and notaries in Paris. Lister and Holden once claimed that they had expended f.3,125,000 (£125,000) on purchasing patents (B-74).

27   See for example, for France, *Bulletin de la Société de l'encouragement pour l'industrie nationale*, volumes for 1840–60 (hereafter *BSEIN*).

28   See Table 3.2.

29   See Chapter 7, pp. 79–87.

30   The money was to be made from licence fees. The strategy was to sell as many machines as possible well in advance of the expiration of the patent. If there were little time left in the life of the patent, prospective purchasers would choose to hang on until it expired.

31   He did not, however, achieve his goal of establishing many factories in Europe.

32   Samuel Lister to Isaac Holden, 1 January 1851 (B-60).

33   *BSEIN* (1845), p. 490. See also *BSEIN* (1846), p. 1076 and *BSEIN* (1848), p. 532.

34   Lister made several visits to St Denis; they were prompted more by difficulties he had with Holden than by interest in the concern. He was using the profits of the concern to build up his English mills.

35   Samuel Lister to Isaac Holden, 22 January 1851 (B-60).

36   Chapter 4, pp. 41–8.

37   Samuel Lister to Isaac Holden, 2 January 1851 (B-60).

38   Lister reported that Schlumberger was advertising in Bradford a reward of £100 for information about the evasion of his patent leading to a conviction (23 January 1851; B-60).

39   It was believed to be particularly well suited to French conditions though could equally well be used in England as subsequent experience showed.

40   J. Burnley, *The History of Wool and Woolcombing* (London, 1889), p. 222.

41   Akroyd and Salt first bought the rights and quickly resold to Lister for the same amount of £30,000 (Burnley, *Wool and Woolcombing*, p. 240). Ironically, the Yorkshire worsted industry now uses a machine comb based on Heilmann's principle and constructed by Schlumberger et cie. of Alsace.

42   Sigsworth, *Black Dyke Mills*, pp. 40–1.

43   These were principally against the Heilmann machine comb.

44   Because of his late entry into French patent purchases, Lister was unlikely to be able to achieve a similarly monopolistic position in France as he had in England.

45   Lister became increasingly committed financially to his English enterprises which he hoped profits from St Denis would pay for; and he became

increasingly anxious about the income from St Denis as the correspondence with Holden indicates. An early example of his anxiety is shown in a letter to Holden in January 1849. 'You must exert yourself to bring the concern up to the greatest possible production...time is too precious, far too precious for delay' (B-59).

46 It not only diverted attention from the Square Motion which Holden wanted to keep secret, but it also provided him with fresh ideas for perfecting the machine comb. Holden could not afford to lay out such sums and was therefore beholden to Lister; his own contribution to the concern was only £300.

47 So inextricably linked were developments in combing on both sides of the Channel, that difficulties arose from English as much as French competitors. This reflected the fact that the worsted industries in these countries were roughly the same size.

48 The trial was held on 9 July 1854 (B-70). There were possibly more trials on this issue as Lister refers to a similar case held on 28 February 1855 (B-62).

49 L-I – Lister and Holden contre Duriez fils.

50 Samuel Lister to Isaac Holden, 9 February 1855 (B-70).

51 L-VII/9.

52 L-I.

53 *Ibid.*

54 Samuel Lister to Isaac Holden, 14 September 1858 (B-65).

55 He patented a feed apparatus in 1856 and specified its use for wool only.

56 The Noble machine comb was equally competent with fine French wools and medium English wools. Lister believed it to be superior to the 'Nip' and the Square Motion machine combs. For example, see Samuel Lister to Isaac Holden, 13 May 1853 (B-61). More information about the use of the Noble machine comb in France is in Chapter 5.

57 Samuel Lister to Isaac Holden, 22 January 1855 (B-62).

58 Throughout the many complex negotiations which ensued, the Heilmann machine comb remained the pivotal concern.

59 Samuel Lister to Isaac Holden 27 April 1855 (B-62).

60 Lister was also anxious to raise funds quickly and offered his share of the St Denis concern to Baron Dufourement and Fould (the Paris banker), who also spurned his offer. (The offer was made on 20 June 1855 (B-70) and rejected on 23 June 1855 (B-62).)

61 Samuel Lister to Issac Holden, 23 April 1855 (B-62).

62 *Ibid.*

63 Samuel Lister to Isaac Holden, 24 April 1855 (B-62).

64 Samuel Lister to Isaac Holden, 10 May 1855 (B-62).

65 Burnley, *Wool and Woolcombing*, p. 379.

66 Samuel Lister to Isaac Holden, July 1856 (B-63).

67 The correspondence is full of unqualified praise for the Noble machine comb. Examples in the letters between Lister and Holden are: 'The Noble machine is the finisher of combing' (4 February 1855; B-62); 'a formidable machine like Noble' (*Ibid.*).

68 Samuel Lister to Isaac Holden, 12 July 1856 (B-63).

69 B-63, *passim.*

70 Samuel Lister to Isaac Holden, 11 June 1856 (B-63).

71 Samuel Lister to Isaac Holden, 15 July 1856 (B-63).

72 *Ibid.*

73 Samuel Lister to Isaac Holden, 16 July 1856 (B-63).

74 Isaac Holden to Sarah Holden, 6 August 1856 (B-27). In October Holden wrote that Schlumberger had agreed to the conditions (29 October 1856; B-27).

75 Samuel Lister to Isaac Holden, 1 November 1856 (B-63).
76 It is not immediately clear why this was, though it later seemed to be because of a pre-existing arrangement between Schlumberger and Tavernier (19 May 1855) (*HIL*, pp. 227, 235). De Molins to Isaac Holden, 19 January 1857 (B-64).
77 This was in an agreement between Donisthorpe and Holden late in 1856 (B-63).
78 John Crofts to Isaac Holden, 3 October 1856 (B-63).
79 *Ibid.* and 13 October 1856. *Ibid.* and B-91/8.
80 That is, he would retain some control over the Noble machine comb.
81 B-91/8.
82 *HIL*, p. 218.
83 *Enquête* (1860), p. 485–7 (L-VIII/2).
84 The licence fee for a Heilmann machine comb was 5000 francs per machine. In order to cover costs, 200 machine combs would need to be sold in the two years before 1860 – an annual rate twice as much as had already been achieved. Chapter 7, p. 79.
85 That is, in the first few years in St Denis.
86 At one stage, Lister demanded that Holden 'throw out all the Square Motions and put in my new machine' (Samuel Lister to Isaac Holden, 23 December 1856 (B-62)).
87 See Chapters 4 and 5, pp. 46–7 and 55–7.
88 Lister's demands were made to fulfil his own inventive activities in England involving the development of another machine comb at his Manningham mill. This was based on the principle of the Hubner machine comb, superior to the Noble machine comb and for use with long and short wool (Samuel Lister to Isaac Holden, 7 November 1857; B-64).
89 Samuel Lister to Isaac Holden, 23 October 1857 (B-64).
90 Holden had also been trying to buy a share in Lister's English concern, but this was finally dropped on 23 December 1858 on which date the official signing of the French agreement took place (B-65).
91 *Enquête industrielle* (1860), p. 480.
92 B-64; for example, Isaac Holden to Harding Cocker (n.d.).
93 B-74.
94 *Ibid.*
95 Details in Chapter 7, *passim.*
96 Holden's desire for a respectable family business was summed up when he wrote: 'I have been working for family. I want an occupation yet for a time and my sons want a business even though ordinary in its return.' (Isaac Holden to Samuel Lister, 23 April 1855, B-62).

4 Establishing the Factories: Success at St Denis 1848-60

Once Lister and Holden recognised a profound common interest in the technical and manufacturing possibilities of mechanical woolcombing, it was natural for them to pool their resources in a joint venture to be located in France. France offered excellent market opportunities as it was Europe's largest worsted producer and its spinning capacity was nearly as great as Britain's.[1] Its worsted industry was based on merino wool which, appropriately, the Square Motion comb handled most efficiently. France also satisfied both men's business aims. Lister entered this venture as part of his plans to expand his manufacturing interests in Europe; Holden, meanwhile, looked upon it as his last and probably best chance to become established in business – at the age of 42, his luck had run out in England and France offered new hope.[2]

In their desire to expand into Europe, Lister and Holden were following previous generations of British entrepreneurs.[3] Unlike their predecessors, however, they did not have the decided advantage of exporting technology from a relatively advanced industrial economy. The level of technical expertise in industrial production in mid-nineteenth-century France was at least as great as it was in Britain. In woolcombing especially, Lister and Holden were entering a highly-charged and competitive environment. Josué Heilmann had just made a major breakthrough in solving the problem of mechanical woolcombing and his machine was being perfected and manufactured by Nicolas Schlumberger, one of the country's leading industrialists. The partners faced an uphill battle. Not only were they attempting to deploy a technology largely unproven under factory conditions; they were also aiming to dominate the French woolcombing industry by controlling or suppressing alternative technologies.

Choosing a suitable factory site was therefore a sensitive matter. On the one hand, the site needed to be close to the main worsted producing areas in order to supply the market efficiently; on the other hand, in the early stages at least, it needed to be sufficiently distant from competitors in the field to protect the technology from potential imitation and infringement of patent rights. Lister, in particular, strongly pressed for a site where secrecy would be assured. In a letter to Holden, he clearly expressed his locational preferences and the reasons for them:[4]

It appears to me if you can take a place out of town it would be better...you would also be less likely to let out your *modus operandi* which I think of great consequence as your keeping exclusive possession of your trade will depend as much upon your keeping your machines secret, as upon the patent. No doubt it will help, but the *best* protection is the *inability* of anyone to imitate you....If you could take some quiet, retired water mill...I think you would find it answers your purpose the best, but it must be near a railway and then distance is nothing, excepting in keeping away inquisitive people.

Lister's insistence on secrecy was direct and clear. Undoubtedly, it was motivated by his entire approach to business which viewed competition in near paranoid terms; but in the matter of locating a factory in France, his position was not only sound but also entirely consistent with the circumstances of French worsted production. The structure of the French worsted industry itself made it difficult to satisfy the first of the conditions of a suitable site. To understand why this was, it is necessary to outline the major features of French worsted production as they emerged during the first half of the nineteenth century.

Until the early 1840s, Paris and Reims dominated French worsted production. The country's first worsted mills were built in Reims and its environs between 1812 and 1825 alongside the older wool mills.[5] Capacity increased rapidly, and Reims quickly dominated the industry specialising in the manufacture of high-quality, pure merino products.[6] In Paris, worsted production grew at an impressive rate before 1840; and at its peak, in the early 1840s, Parisian spinning capacity accounted for approximately 10 per cent of total French worsted spindlage. This predominance was short-lived, however, and systematic contraction followed the peak of the early 1840s.[7] In the development and diffusion of technology and fashion, however, Paris continued to exert an influence on the industry.[8]

As mechanised spinning became increasingly applied to the worsted industry, additional areas of production emerged.[9] As production in Paris declined absolutely, growth occurred in Alsace, Fourmies, Le Cateau, Roubaix and Tourcoing.[10] The nature of production in these areas, however, differed considerably. In Alsace, predominantly a cotton-producing area, the industry was technically more advanced and organisationally more sophisticated than elsewhere.[11] Fourmies was the smallest worsted producing area, and unlike other parts of France, where worsted production was part of a large textile (and industrial) sector, Fourmies specialised in this activity.[12] The worsted industry in Le Cateau, by contrast, was dominated by the highly integrated concern of Paturle-Lupin, purported to be the largest worsted mill in the country.[13]

The development of Fourmies and Le Cateau as worsted producing centres before 1850, however, was overshadowed quantitatively by the expansion in Roubaix and Tourcoing. Roubaix – the Bradford of France – had been, during the eighteenth century, an important producer of both wool and cotton. Diversification into worsted production began in the early 1830s, and in the following twenty years was the fastest growing industrial activity in Roubaix, and had become the largest concentration of worsted spinning in France.[14] Roubaix did not develop its own combing sector before mid-century and relied entirely on Tourcoing for its supply of combed wool.

Tourcoing – France's equivalent of Halifax – traditionally specialised in the production of combed wool, which it initially exported to spinning mills throughout France.[15] By 1850, however, all of its combed wool was absorbed by the mills in the locality of the two cities.[16]

In the early years of expansion, therefore, worsted production spread to many parts of France. Activity in Paris and Reims provided much of the foundation of the subsequent development of the industry, but otherwise, and certainly until the 1830s, there was no clear pattern or consistency to French worsted production.[17] This changed in the twenty years to 1850 when the decline of productive activity in Paris was accompanied by an impressive expansion and concentration of production in the Nord *département* (including Fourmies, Le Cateau, Roubaix and Tourcoing), and in Reims, and the emergence of Alsace as the predominant worsted machine-making area. By 1850, therefore, worsted production was becoming concentrated in three or four main areas, but even then, a significant proportion of the industry's capacity was decentralised.[18] In this respect, the structure of the French worsted industry differed fundamentally from its British counterpart, where Bradford alone accounted for the vast majority of the country's output.

In September 1848, Holden travelled to Paris accompanied by Lister's French agent, Ferdinand Tavernier, to search for a factory site near the city.[19] They found a suitable site in Corbeil, to the south of Paris, but for unknown reasons Holden failed to complete the purchase of the property. The search resumed, and in February of the following year, Holden arranged to rent a factory in St Denis, to the north of Paris.[20]

St Denis was, in many ways, a perfect location for Lister and Holden's woolcombing operations.[21] The town was an important industrial centre; its economic structure was varied and included sizeable textile, metal and chemical industries.[22] Textile production, especially cotton printing, expanded rapidly in the two decades before Holden's arrival. According to official sources, the number of firms in the textile industry increased from 33 to 59 and the labour force employed rose from 964 to 2539 in the period 1840 to 1856.[23]

The factory site itself, called Le Grand Barrage, became available for rent by an ironic turn of events, and turned out to suit their specific needs perfectly. During the 1830s, John Cockerill, one of the leading European industrialists of the time, occupied the site, first with a cotton weaving and printing factory, and then with a worsted mill.[24] In 1838, Cockerill sold the site to Juliana Collier, widow of John Collier, who developed it for manufacturing woolcombing and weaving machinery originally of her husband's design.[25] Part of the site was rented in the 1840s to Bernier-Thibout, another designer and producer of wool-combing machinery.[26] After a few years of successful business, Madame Collier suffered a series of misfortunes; a fire, two bankruptcies and an unscrupulously dishonest partner finally led to her downfall. In 1848, the factory ceased production though the winding-up process took a further ten years to complete: in the meantime, the premises were available for rent.[27]

In addition to the advantages of its industrial structure and the specific features of the factory site, St Denis was an admirable location in being so near Paris. Though worsted production was in decline, Paris, as we have seen, remained an important centre for technical innovation, design and fashion. Partly because of that, and partly because of the concentration of financial and commercial institutions in the city, many prominent worsted manufacturers had a branch of their business in Paris. Finally, Paris was the centre of all legal matters relating to patents – a fact of great consequence considering Lister and Holden's deep involvement in complex patent negotiations and battles.[28]

The site alone could only partially guarantee the degree of secrecy Lister, in particular, wanted.[29] To protect the technology further, Holden took the following measures. First, he imported the wool-combing machines, machine parts and replacements from England. In exceptional circumstances, he had parts made in France, but these were always by English firms resident there.[30] Secondly, he tried to ensure the greatest loyalty from his workforce by recruiting British workers for the most responsible positions in the firm (managers, foremen, mechanics, etc.) and, being a deeply committed Methodist himself, those with strong nonconformist leanings. Holden experienced little difficulty in achieving this aim. Within a few months of opening the factory, Holden was receiving many letters requesting work.[31] The necessary personnel were recruited, and within a year or two, St Denis had the makings of a reasonably-sized British community.[32] Holden provided the community with a chapel, regular Bible classes and the benefits of a Mutual Improvement Society which he founded.[33] In short, Holden had become the archetypal paternalistic factory owner.

Lister and Holden were thus very methodical and careful in establishing themselves in France. Nothing was left to chance. Even St

Denis's main disadvantage as a site – its isolation from the country's main worsted producing areas – was overcome. The accessibility of railway transport and the proximity of Paris helped solve the problem of distance. As to making business contacts in the French worsted industry, a problem compounded by St Denis's remoteness from the market, Lister enlisted the help of Baron de Fourment, one of France's leading and most influential worsted manufacturers.[34] De Fourment was indispensable to the firm in its early years.[35] Thanks to him, Holden quickly acquainted himself with market conditions, and by the beginning of 1850 was producing combed wool for important worsted spinners in Alsace, Roubaix and Fourmies.[36]

In establishing their joint concern in France, Lister clearly provided much of the inspiration and certainly all of the valuable contacts. Yet success could only be achieved by a determined effort to provide the French market with the best possible combed wool. This was Holden's main responsibility.

The original partnership agreement between Holden and Lister was drawn up in October 1848. Although Holden's initial contribution amounted to only £300, the partners were to have 'an equal interest and share in the profits of the concern' (this later changed to a division of 2:1 in Lister's favour.)[37] A further clause in the contract stated that Lister was to provide his patented combing machines, while Holden was to take responsibility for managing the firm. For this role he was guaranteed a yearly salary of £200, but the actual remuneration was to be tied to profits.[38] It was agreed that Holden was to be committed to the St Denis plant and to perfecting the operation of his Square Motion machine there, while Lister would be based in Bradford and free to develop other interests. Ferdinand Tavernier, already Lister's French agent for several years, was to continue in the role and provide Holden with useful contacts in the French worsted industry.[39]

The 1848 agreement between Holden and Lister was broad in scope and general in terms. When Holden travelled to France that year, the precise nature of the enterprise that he and his partner envisaged was far from fully formulated. They were committed to the mechanical combing of wool, but neither the technique to be employed nor the organisation of production had been fully discussed. In terms of approach to production the effective choice was between commission combing, which was the practice at Lister's Manningham mills, and top producing. It was the principle of commission combing that the customer, typically a worsted spinner, provided the comber with raw wool and later received this processed and separated into top and noil. The practice of commission combing had existed in France in the handcombing sector, though top selling, where the purchase of the raw material was the responsibility of the comber, was probably more popular.[40]

Commission combing was preferred by the partners for several reasons: it was familiar to them; it required a modicum of working capital; turnover was rapid; and in France, they believed, less competition would be encountered. It was decided that production at St Denis would take this form in the short term: 'The French concern was started altogether upon the principle of commission combing...my idea has always been to do as we did at Manningham...commission work...and as the concern made capital to employ it in top making.[41] There was also a strong suggestion that some of the St Denis plant capacity was to be used to supply top to the Bradford market, combing either French or English wool depending on its cost.[42]

The partners' effective choice of machinery lay between the 'Nip' and the Square Motion.[43] Trials of each machine were held at St Denis, and although Holden and Lister never agreed on the relative merits of the two within the French worsted industry, Holden, with more immediate control over the operations at the St Denis concern, ensured that his own machine was employed. Despite the obvious contribution of the Square Motion comb to the success of the French enterprise, Lister resented Holden's choice for the duration of the partnership.[44]

From the outset, the partnership was, at best, uneasy. The different aspirations of the two men and incompatible perceptions of how these might best be achieved became quickly apparent.[45] Lister was anxious to move fast, whereas Holden was content to proceed gradually and to found a solid business. Lister diversified his activities and enterprises, while his partner was committed to the St Denis concern and to the Square Motion machine.[46] It was probably Lister's urgent desire for cash that determined the policy of commission combing at St Denis, and it was his incessant capital requirements that ensured its continuation. Lister was more immediately concerned with his mills in Yorkshire and Germany,[47] and while he wished to expand further into Europe, he initially took his share of the profits from the French firm to maintain the Manningham plant.[48] He advised Holden frequently on management and control of the business; and exhortations to improve performance became commonplace: 'You must exert yourself to bring the concern up to the greatest possible production combined with perfect work'; 'If you cannot succeed I shall certainly take the concern underhand myself. Time is too precious, far too precious for delay.'[49]

Lister's heavy financial commitments elsewhere became a major source of tension between the two partners. A further focus of explicit discord was the role of Ferdinand Tavernier. There is no doubt that Tavernier and the Baron de Fourment smoothed the path of the infant enterprise and ensured the regular flow of custom upon which the success of commission combing depended. Lister, however, overestimated Tavernier's worth and frequently bestowed rewards upon him, while

Holden, who more accurately appraised the Frenchman's talent, resented his troublesome presence.[50] This, and other early disagreements between the two men, remained unresolved, and caused increasing friction during the ten-year partnership.[51]

The St Denis business, though turbulent, was successful.[52] Organisationally and technically it was unique. The Square Motion comb, once in full-time operation, produced high-quality top with little waste. The reputation of the firm for consistently superior output spread rapidly beyond the original customers, and the early success of the St Denis enterprise was reflected in the £10,000 turnover during the first six months of 1851, when 338,000 kg of top was produced.[53]

Despite the evident achievement of the St Denis factory under Holden's control, Lister persisted in his demands for the 'Nip' to be employed in France and for commission combing to be replaced by top production once sufficient capital was available.[54] He was also unhappy with Holden's style of management: 'I feel I have never made a greater mistake than in placing you at the head of a concern, your conduct is shameful.'[55] To alleviate Lister's disquiet and to dissipate the tension caused by Tavernier's presence, a new mill site was sought, late in 1851, in the Nord.[56] The mill would be managed by Tavernier and would produce top by means of the 'Nip' machine. Holden would thus be left in peace to perfect his Square Motion comb and to pursue his own preferred method of production: 'I propose to have a concern at Lille and to relieve you of the burden and annoyance of Mr. Tavernier, leaving you Reims, Paris and indeed all of France except the neighbourhood of Lille.'[57]

By 1851 expansion was certainly appropriate, and both Holden and Lister felt sufficiently prepared to expose their business practices to the competition of the major French worsted producing regions.[58] By December of that year it had been agreed to place Tavernier at the head of a factory at Lille, and to establish a further enterprise in Reims under the management of Holden's nephew, Jonathan Holden.[59] While the proposed Reims mill constituted genuine expansion, Lister's objective in setting up business in Lille was to prove the worth of his 'Nip' machine, as well as to quell the bickering of Holden and Tavernier:

I have done all I can to make both your position and that of Mr. Tavernier comfortable and profitable and the end of it is neither of you are pleased, although both of you (considering that neither had a shilling when you came to me) are in splendid positions if only you know when to be content.[60]

The search for a mill site near Lille proved fruitless and was abandoned in 1852. Business at St Denis continued to prosper, and by the end of the year, on Lister's instigation, a factory site was found near

Roubaix and the construction of extensive factory premises there and at Reims was in progress.[61] The choice of sites for the extension to the Lister and Holden enterprise had been carefully considered. The partners had decided on Croix, a small settlement on the outskirts of Roubaix in the Nord.[62] It was situated in the heart of the French textile belt, yet was secluded from potential and actual competitors.

Reims by contrast was a large and well-established wool and worsted-producing town within the Marne textile region.[63] The Lister and Holden factory, however, was sited on the fringes of the town, and isolated from their major competitors. Production began at both factories in 1853 – Croix under the management of another nephew, Isaac Crothers, and Reims directed by Jonathan Holden.

Between 1853 and 1859 all three factories operated simultaneously, though Lister's involvement, even in St Denis, became increasingly tenuous. Lister made several attempts during the early 1850s to dispose of his share in the partnership despite the considerable sums he was earning from it.[64] The St Denis enterprise flourished during the mid 1850s; the output and profit levels are shown in Table 4.1. In 1853, the plant's machinery had been valued at £43,299,[65] and in mid-1854, Lister calculated his share of the business to be worth £70,000.[66] Holden's nurturing of his invention and of the enterprise, therefore, led to remarkable success. He was immediately responsible for the direction of the St Denis enterprise, because, although Lister frequently offered advice, it was typically rejected. Holden was nevertheless indebted to Lister for his initial capital investment and for his aid in protecting the Square Motion machine; indeed, the exceptional degree of commercial success was attributable to the distinct, yet complementary skills of the two partners. Holden gained his reputation through a clear understanding of the French industrial situation and through a confidence in the economic validity of his machine which, by the mid-1850s, was producing the results he had anticipated.[67] Lister's role in the short term as provider of capital and experience should not be undervalued, while the long-term impact of his patent purchasing activities was incalculable.

During 1857, while the factories at Croix and Reims sustained impressive growth rates, it was becoming clear that the St Denis enterprise was running out of steam. The poor performance was not a temporary set-back attributable to the world-wide financial and business crisis.[68] The partnership between Holden and Lister was deteriorating; and the latter, under growing financial strain, began to alienate his partner. Because of the great success achieved by his nephews at Croix and Reims, together with Lister's indifference, Holden began to contemplate a genuine family empire. To fulfil his desire to purchase Lister's interest in the business, Holden began to

Table 4.1: The St Denis business, 1851-60

	Output (kg)	Unit cost (f/kg)	Unit price (f/kg)	Profit (f)
1851	591,500	—	—	—
1853	879,000	—	1.5	—
1854	811,800	—	1.5	—
1855	969,755	0.97	1.43	533,781
1856	564,465	1.19	1.21	135,280
1859	—	—	—	-13,000
1860	production ceased			

Sources: L-I; L-VII/7, 10; B-69; B-91/5; B-91/6

resist his partner's requests for cash and to reinforce Lister's immediate position of economic weakness:[69]

> The creditors give him very readily it seems two years to pay in. I learn, however, that some of them are very dissatisfied with the arrangement at bottom ... Lister said that he would still find it difficult to meet payments in the other two concerns.... I have firmly refused either to give money or security unless he gives me half of the concern at St Denis. He would not concede that but I think I shall bring him to.[70]

Holden was supported in this action by his son Angus, who urged Isaac to turn Lister's predicament to his advantage: 'Offer Lister a low figure - if he does not sell now wait for his creditors to get him'.[71] Angus's resentment of Lister for undermining his father's ability and for making his life difficult found frequent expression: 'has he not since the commencement done all he could to thwart your projects and do you all the injury he could... and then trying to sell his concern... to Donisthorpe and trying to throw you out'; 'all his plans and schemes have fallen through - his English concerns conducted on his principle are bankrupt and in spite of all the *ennui* he has caused you, the French concerns are in a flourishing condition.'[72] Holden was unsuccessful in assuming sole control of the French enterprises during 1857, but in the following year he actively pursued the withdrawal of Lister by refusing him the cash for which he was increasingly desperate.[73]

Since the establishment of the mills at Reims and Croix, Holden had been running down the St Denis business in order to direct capital into the newer plants and so accelerate their growth. By 1858, the French worsted industry had become more clearly concentrated in the Nord and the Marne; and the role of Paris, even as a technical locus, had become peripheral. The St Denis plant had successfully served its purpose as an experimental base, but the future of the Holden empire clearly lay in the mainstream of French woolcombing.

Lister, aware of the large accumulations of capital generated by the St Denis business and frustrated by his inability to obtain a share of it, attempted to reduce Holden's power by admitting Donisthorpe and Crofts to a fifth share of Lister and Holden.[74] This action served only to strengthen Holden's resolve to gain sole control over the French enterprises, and also to purchase shares in Lister's English concerns. Angus, however, persuaded his father against this latter course: 'If I were you I would just let Mr. Lister and his wondrous combing patents go to where he liked.'[75] Holden took his son's advice, and was soon able to buy Lister's share of the French concerns for £74,000, from which Lister paid Holden £11,250 for the release of Donisthorpe and Crofts.[76] Holden remained at St Denis for a further two years before finally winding up the business in November 1860. He then returned to England to oversee his new factory, Penny Oak, at Bradford; and although he left his nephews in charge of the Croix and Reims factories, he remained in overall control.[77]

The decade at St Denis had provided Holden (and to a lesser extent Lister) with valuable experience. Between 1849 and 1860 Holden had experimented with and then perfected his Square Motion machine without fear of intruders or imitators. He had developed new methods of operation and was able to conclude that commission combing was, for him, the most efficient use of resources. Commission combing had been chosen initially because of its low working capital requirements, but was found to provide such a rapid return on capital that it was never replaced.[78] Having established a formula for success, the technical and organisational features were replicated at Croix and Reims, and the growth of those factories was accelerated by the surplus generated by St Denis.

Notes

1 In 1850, there were 800,000 worsted spindles in France and 864,750 in Britain. Germany, the next largest European worsted producer, had 300,000 spindles. D. Landes, *The Unbound Prometheus* (Cambridge, 1969), pp. 173, 212; and *Exposition Universelle de 1851: Travaux de la commission française* (Paris, 1854), vol. IV, p. 155.

2 In a letter to his wife Sarah, Holden explained why he was in France in the following way: 'Providence I believe has called me here. As a man of business I enter into the most inviting openings that Providence places before me and there remain, with contented mind, till Providence again directs my path into a course more desirable' (10 January 1851; *HIL*, p. 161).

3 W.O. Henderson, *Britain and Industrial Europe, 1750–1870* (Leicester, 1972).

4 B–58. Examples of similar advice can be found in B–59 – Lister to Holden January, and 13 February 1849.

5 Guillaume Ternaux, France's leading woollen manufacturer at the beginning of the nineteenth century, is credited with laying the foundations of modern French worsted production when he installed mules for worsted spinning in a mill in Bazancourt, near Reims, in 1812. The mill was owned jointly by Ternaux (whose base was Paris) and his brother-in-law, Jobert-Lucas, a prominent Reims manufacturer. Ternaux was a remarkable entrepreneur whose interests ranged widely over economic and political matters. He owned several woollen mills in Sedan, Louviers, Elbeuf, Leghorn and Naples; he also had an important textile machine workshop in Paris which made significant contributions to the advancement of textile technology and thereby enhanced the reputation of Paris in this field. Ternaux was also involved in cloth developments where he was particularly successful in mixing silk with cashmere. But more than this, Ternaux is credited with what was probably the most important aspect of French worsted production – its predominant and early use of pure merino wool. Ternaux became interested in merino wool as a possible substitute for and imitation of the fibres commonly used in the production of relatively expensive Far Eastern cloth which was in vogue in the early decades of the century. He chose the area near Reims as the location of a worsted spinning concern because Reims was the centre of the Champagne merino wool trade. See L. Bergeron, 'Douglas, Ternaux, Cockerill: aux origines de la mécanisation de l'industrie lainière en France', *Revue Historique*, 247 (1972), pp. 67–80. For more information on Jobert-Lucas, see G. Clause, 'L'industrie lainière rémoise a l'époque napoléonienne', *Revue d'histoire moderne et contemporaine*, 17 (1970), pp. 574–95; C. Ballot, *L'introduction du machinisme dans l'industrie française* (Paris, 1923), pp. 35, 198–9; W. O. Henderson, *Britain and Industrial Europe, 1750–1870* (Leicester, 1972), p. 31; A. L. Dunham, *The Industrial Revolution in France, 1815–1848* (New York, 1955), pp. 342–3, 430; M. Lévy-Leboyer, *Les Banques européennes et l'industrialisation internationale dans la première moitié du XIXe siècle* (Paris, 1964), pp. 120, 124; M. Alcan, *Fabrication des étoffes: Traité du travail des laines peignées* (Paris, 1873), pp. 44–5. For Ternaux's plans for merino flocks in the Champagne, see *ADM*, 187 M17; Dunham, *The Industrial Revolution*, pp. 152–4, 344; C. Moreau-Berillon, *Le Mouton en Champagne* (Paris, 1909).

6 *ADM*, 187 M17; Bergeron, 'Douglas, Ternaux, Cockerill', pp. 67–80; Clause, 'L'industrie lainière', pp. 574–95. Between 1800 and 1850, the total value of woollen and worsted cloth increased from 11 million francs to 45 million francs; total spinning capacity increased from 41,800 spindles in 1829 to 270,000 spindles in 1850. See *ADM*, 186 M12; *Exposition universelle à Vienne, 1873. Chambre de Commerce de Reims: Notes sur Reims et le département de la Marne*, pp. 6–7. The figures on spindlage are from *ADM*, 187 M17 for 1829, and *Exposition Universelle de 1851*, p. 15 for 1850. Before 1850, Reims worsted spinners collected most of the prizes in the competitions for yarn held at the French exhibitions in 1834, 1839 and 1849. For notes on the prize-winners, see C. Dupin. *Rapport du Jury Central sur les produits de l' industrie française exposés en 1834* (Paris, 1836), vol. 2, pp. 17–19; *Exposition des produits de l'industrie française en 1839: Rapport du Jury Central* (Paris, 1839), vol. 1, pp. 29–37, vol. 2, pp. 30–1; *Rapport du Jury Central sur les produits de l'agriculture et de l'industrie exposés en 1849* (Paris, 1850), vol. 3, pp. 6–11.

7 Data on worsted spinning capacity in Paris between 1827 and 1861 are:

Table 4.2: Worsted spinning capacity in Paris 1827–61

	Number of spindles	Number of firms
1827	10,000	7
1834	20,000	7
1839	60,000	10
1848	42,270	13
1861	29,660	?

Sources: 1827, 1834, 1839: *Exposition des Produits de l'industrie française en 1839: Rapport du Jury Central* (Paris, 1839), I, p. 29. 1848: *Statistique de l'industrie à Paris* (Paris, 1851), pp. 369–70. 1861: *Statistique de la France*, 1861–65 (Nancy, 1873) pp. xx–xxi.

8   Apart from Ternaux, the names of William Douglas and John Collier are most often associated with the role of Paris as a centre for textile technology. Important contributions in the field included cloth-shearing and spinning equipment, carding machines, and the machine comb (perfected by John Collier). In the 1840s, Paris was an important centre of mechanically- produced combed wool in contrast to the rest of the country where handcombing predominated. See Henderson, *Britain and Industrial Europe*, pp. 31, 59, 63; *Exposition Universelle de 1851: Travaux de la commission française* (Paris, 1854), vol. IV, pp. 175–91; Lévy-Leboyer, *Les Banques*, pp. 119–21; Dunham, *The Industrial Revolution*, pp. 288–9; *Statistique de l'industrie à Paris* (Paris, 1851) pp. 415–18. For Paris as a centre of fashion and textile design, see *Exposition Universelle de 1851*, pp. 175–91; Dunham, *The Industrial Revolution*, pp. 281, 339–43.

9   *Exposition Universelle de 1851*, pp. 152–3.

10 The Paris cotton industry had a similar experience earlier in the nineteenth century. See D. Pinkney, 'Paris, capitale du coton sous le premier empire', *Annales: E.S.C.* (1950), pp. 56–60. In 1815, Paris had 50 cotton mills with a capacity of 150,000 spindles; around 1848, the corresponding figures were 12 mills with 56,020 spindles. C. Fohlen, *L'industrie textile au temps du second empire* (Paris, 1956), p. 161; and *Statistique de l'industrie à Paris*, p. 367; Lévy-Leboyer, *Les Banques*, pp. 58–9.

11 Many worsted mills were owned by cotton manufacturers. Power looms, spinning machinery and other accessories of the worsted industry were manufactured by leading textile machine-makers such as André Koechlin and Nicolas Schlumberger whose interests ranged over textiles as well as other industries. See *Histoire documentaire de l'industrie de Mulhouse et de ses environs au XIXe siècle* (Mulhouse, 1902), pp. 472–3; Dunham, *The Industrial Revolution*, pp. 251, 262, 276–7, 432; Fohlen, *L'industrie textile*, pp. 105, 454; *Enquête sur le régime économique* (Paris, 1870), vol. 2, p. 248. Worsted spinning capacity between 1844 and 1871 is shown in the table below which also reveals the degree of concentration.

Table 4.3: Worsted spinning capacity in Alsace, 1844–71

	Number of spindles	Number of firms	Average capacity (spindles per firm)
1844	9,600	2	4,800
1848	28,000	4	7,000
1855	46,000	6	7,667
1861	71,500	6	11,920
1871	104,410	4	26,102

Sources: 1844, 1848: M. Lévy-Leboyer, *Les Banques européenes et l'industrialisation internationale* (Paris, 1964) p. 163. 1855: *Bulletin de la société industrielle de Mulhouse*, 26–7 (1855) p. 388. 1861: S. Pollard and C. Holmes, *Documents of European Economic History* (London, 1968), I, p. 309. 1870: *Histoire documentaire de l'industrie de Mulhouse et de ses environs au XIXe siècle* (Mulhouse, 1902) p. 1005.

By way of contrast, it was not until the 1870s that mills in Fourmies and Roubaix were similar in spindlage to those in Alsace in 1848. See *Enquête* (1870), p. 246 and *ADN*, M653/44.

12   The population of Fourmies in 1851 was 3,360; that of Reims 43,643; and that of Roubaix 34,698. *Annuaire Statistique du Département du Nord* (1952); *Statistique de la France: Résultats du dénombrement de la population en 1856* p. xx. Lévy-Leboyer, *Les Banques*, p. 127.

13   The mill began operations in 1818. In 1844, it had a capacity of 25,000 spindles accounting for half of the worsted spindlage in the Fourmies–Le Cateau region. The mill was largely self-contained and was one of the first in France to experiment with mechanical combing. See A. Falleur, *L'industrie lainière dans la région de Fourmies* (Paris, 1930), pp. 20–1, 25–6; *ADN*, M547/5.

14   Lévy-Leboyer, *Les Banques*, p. 167; M. Raman, 'Mesure de la croissance d'un centre textile: Roubaix de 1789 à 1913', *Revue d'histoire économique et sociale*, 51 (1973), pp. 476, 480, 482, 499–500. Many cotton mills were re-equipped for worsted spinning in 1837 and 1839. Fohlen, *L'Industrie textile*, pp. 94–6; T. Leuridan, *Histoire de Roubaix* (Roubaix, 1864), vol. 5, pp. 148, 156. The rapidity with which the entrepreneurs of Roubaix shifted between cotton and worsted is given prominence in accounting for Roubaix's rapid rise in textile production. See, for example, C. Fohlen, 'Esquisse d'une évolution industrielle: Roubaix au XIXe siècle', *Revue du Nord* 33 (1951), pp. 92–102; and D. Landes, 'Religion and Enterprise: The Case of the French Textile Industry', in E.C. Carter, R. Forster, and J.N. Moody, *Enterprise and Entrepreneurs in Nineteenth- and Twentieth-Century France* (London, 1976), pp. 41–86. The claim is based on data in the following sources: Lévy-Leboyer, *Les Banques*, p. 167; Raman, 'Mesure de la Croissance', p. 482; *Statistique de la France* (Paris, 1847), vol. 1, pp. 40–3.

15   Lévy-Leboyer, *Les Banques*, p. 166; Fohlen, 'Esquisse d'une évolution', p. 96.

16   Estimated from data in the following: *ADN*, M547/5; *Statistique de la France: Industrie. Résultats généraux de l'enquête 1861–65* (Nancy, 1873), p.

XLIX; A. Chanut *et al.*, 'Aspects industriels de la crise: le département du Nord', in E. Labrousse, *Aspects de la crise et de la dépression de l'économie française au milieu du XIXe siècle, 1846-1851* (La Roche-sur-Yon, 1956), p. 97.

17   For comparison with conditions in Britain, where worsted production was highly localised, see D. T. Jenkins and K. G. Ponting, *The British Wool Textile Industry* (London, 1982), pp. 30, 77–80, 177.

18   In 1850, Fourmies, Reims and Roubaix-Tourcoing accounted for 10, 15 and 23 per cent, respectively, of France's total capacity of 800,000 worsted spindles. Calculated from Falleur, *L'Industrie lainière*, p. 25; *Exposition Universelle de 1851*, p. 194; *ADN*, M547/5; Raman, 'Mesure de la croissance', p. 482.

19   L-I. There is no evidence in any extant material relating to Holden that a location other than one near Paris was ever seriously considered.

20   According to a letter from Lister to Holden, Tavernier had reached an agreement with the owners of the mill site in Corbeil (3 November; B–58). It is clear from a subsequent letter in January of the following year, however, that the matter had not been as straightforward as first believed, and indeed, that the deal had fallen through (B–59). The St Denis site was agreed upon by at least 12 February 1849 (B–59).

21   Years later, Holden was to refer to the operation at St Denis as an error of judgement, but there is little doubt that he was expressing only the bitterness he felt about a subsequent episode with Lister. See Holden's comments about locating business in France in 'Retrospective Notes in Reference to Combing and Combing Establishments', p. 8 (B–77). See also the negative comments on the St Denis site made in Henderson, *Britain and Industrial Europe*, p. 84.

22   J.-F. Nicol, 'L'industrialisation de la commune de St Denis dans la seconde moitié du 19e siècle' (thèse maitresse, Université de Paris X, 1972). St Denis was the site of the first factory producing soda by the Leblanc method. J. G. Smith, *The Origins and Early Development of the Heavy Chemical Industry in France* (Oxford, 1979), pp. 215–35, 230–40, 244–6.

23   Nicol, 'L'industrialisation', pp. 64, 65; *AMSD*, F 3/8/3/1. In 1851, the civilian population of St Denis stood at 13,688.

24   Lévy-Leboyer, *Les Banques*, p. 161, 655. For Cockerill generally, see *ibid.*, *passim*; and Henderson, *Britain and Industrial Europe*, *passim*. See also *AMSD*, F 3/4/3/2 and 3/10/7/4.

25   *AMSD*, F 3/4/3/2.

26   In a patent granted on 15 November 1845, Bernier-Thibout was styled as 'Peigneurs de laine au Grand Barrage à St Denis', *Catalogue des Brevets d'invention* (1844–46).

27   ADS, $D^{10}U^3/26$, 7419; J. J. Hémardinquer, 'Une dynastie de mécaniciens anglais en France: James, John et Juliana Collier (1791–1847)', *Revue d'histoire des sciences et de leurs applications*, 17 (1964), p. 203.

28   See Chapter 3 for Lister and Holden's legal activities.

29   On the importance of secrecy generally, see P. Mathias, 'Skills and the Diffusion of Innovations from Britain in the Eighteenth Century', *Transactions of the Royal Historical Society*, 5th ser., 25 (1975), pp. 111–13.

30   For Holden's import of machinery into France see *AN*, F12 4803–11. The English firms in France included Harding Cocker and J. Ward in Lille and Malo-Dickson in Dunkirk; in England, they included Taylor Wordsworth in Leeds and Hattersley in Bradford.

31   Examples of letters requesting work can be found in L–VI/9 and 10. Apparently, Holden paid the passage to France.

32 *AMSD*, F 3/8/3/1. 67 British nationals were enumerated in the 1851 census.
33 *HIL*, p. 822. The first regular preacher in St Denis was Charles Faulkner, formerly a mechanic at the factory and subsequently the minister at Croix for many years. His daughter Fanny married Isaac Holden Crothers, Holden's nephew. See Isaac Holden to Sarah Holden, 15 August 1853 (B–24); Charles Faulkner to Isaac Holden, 27 August 1857 (L–VII/8); letter of introduction from Richard Watts, temporary Chaplain in Lille 2 May 1859 in Papers of the French Mission, Lambeth Palace Library, London. For the religious life of the St Denis community generally, see E. Jennings, 'Sir Isaac Holden (1807–1897): "The First Comber in Europe"' (PhD, University of Bradford, 1982), pp. 61–4.
34 For de Fourment, see *Dictionnaire de Biographie Française* (Paris, 1979), vol. XIV, p. 783; *Exposition Universelle de 1851*, p. 152; *Statistique de la France* (Paris, 1847), vol. I, p. 86. At the time of the industrial census in the early 1840s, de Fourment was employing 1066 persons spinning and weaving merino wool at his mill in Cercamp, Pas-de-Calais. The spinning capacity of the mill was 18,908 spindles: the largest worsted mill in the country – Paturle-Lupin in Le Cateau – had 24,000 spindles at the same time.
35 See B–91/3 for a list of Holden's early customers. See also, Isaac Holden to Sarah Holden, 4 September 1850 (B–21); *ibid.*, 8 October 1852, (B–23); *ibid.*, 29 February 1852 (B–23); and L–VII/1.
36 Holden also sought out customers by demonstrating the excellent quality of yarn produced from his combed wool and spun on imported machinery in his factory. *AN*, F12, 4803–4811.
37 The first draft agreement was dated 25 October 1848; the final agreement was made on 1 July 1849. Aside from the change in the distribution of profits, no other changes of substance were made between these dates. See B–58, B–59 and Lister to Holden, 3 July 1849 (B–59).
38 *Ibid.*
39 These were vital for successful commission combing. Lister was confident that the Baron de Fourment 'would send you as much commission work as you liked' (B–59).
40 There would be more control over production but greater capital input required for a longer period.
41 Samuel Lister to Isaac Holden, 22 May 1849 (B–59).
42 'If the wool is found to be cheaper here than in France and better adapted to machine work I will keep you supplied.' Samuel Lister to Isaac Holden, 30 May 1849 (B–59).
43 See Chapter 3, pp. 26–34.
44 *Ibid.*
45 *Ibid.*
46 *Ibid.*
47 *Ibid.*
48 Letters between Lister and Holden throughout 1849 in B–59.
49 *Ibid.*
50 B–59 and B–60.
51 See Chapter 3, pp. 28–33.
52 The first half-yearly earnings reached £10,000 (18 June 1851; B–60). Subsequently profits approached £50,000 per annum, then expansion by ploughing-back profits was rapid.
53 L–VII/7.
54 Lister admonished Holden frequently for wasting time on perfecting the Square Motion: 'the Square Motion has nothing to it' (8 January 1851; B–60). Commission combing was less profitable than top production and

had been introduced as a temporary expedient. It was safe in an uncertain political climate and required only a small capital outlay and thus was necessary for only a short time. Within months Lister was suggesting a shift to top production, and continued to do so (because of his partner's recalcitrance) until shortly before the partnership ended in 1858.

55   Samuel Lister to Isaac Holden, 26 July 1851 (B-60).
56   Samuel Lister to Isaac Holden, 8 November 1851 (B-60): it was mentioned several times but finally shelved.
57   Samuel Lister to Isaac Holden, 6 December 1851 (B-60).
58   'it is determined to have new mills at Lille and Reims.' Samuel Lister to Isaac Holden, 8 November 1851 (B-60).
59   Samuel Lister to Isaac Holden, 6 December 1851 (B-60).
60   *Ibid.*
61   *HIL*, p. 172.
62   Jean Piat, *Croix: Dix siècles d'histoire* (Croix, 1972), p. 49. For the social and economic development of Croix during the second half of the nineteenth century, see K. Honeyman and J. Goodman, 'Un industriel anglais et la ville de Croix, 1850–1900', in P. Delsalle (ed), *Manufactures et Entreprises*, (forthcoming Tourcoing, 1986).
63   In 1872, two-thirds of all cloth produced in Reims was worsted. US Department of State: Commercial Relations of the United States, *Cotton and Woolen Mills in Europe: Report from the Consuls of the U.S.*, 23 September 1882 (Washington, 1882), p. 157.
64   For example, Samuel Lister to Isaac Holden, 23 April 1855 (B-62); though during 1854 his immediate financial worries were allayed by a lucrative marriage (Isaac Holden to Sarah Holden, 2 August 1854; B-25).
65   Information contained in a letter from Tavernier to Lister, 13 July 1854 (B-69).
66   Samuel Lister to Isaac Holden, 25 June 1854 (B-69).
67   The machine was clearly very efficient and contributed to low operating costs and high profits. As early as 1853, Holden had been prepared to buy out Lister for £67,000 (B-91/5).
68   Though this clearly had an impact on Lister, particularly as he was apparently over-extending himself financially.
69   Holden was clearly beginning to work on another course of action.
70   Isaac Holden to Sarah Holden, 25 December 1857 (B-28).
71   Angus Holden to Isaac Holden, 21 December 1857 (L-VII/8).
72   *Ibid.*
73   In a letter to Holden, Lister asked where the accumulated capital was going (1 January 1858; B-65).
74   Samuel Lister to Isaac Holden, end January 1858 (B-65).
75   Edward Holden to Isaac Holden, 27 October 1858 (B-65).
76   See Chapter 4 and B-91/9.
77   He also made frequent tours of inspection of his French factories.
78   Indeed by the 1850s, Holden did control the largest commission combing enterprise in Europe and the influence of the Holden enterprise was to grow steadily during the nineteenth century.

5 Isaac Holden et Fils: The Performance of the Factories in Croix and Reims, 1852–1901

Before production ceased at St Denis, the factories at both Croix and Reims had become well established. During the 1850s their expansion was rapid through the retention of profits and the diversion of surplus capital from St Denis. Output figures for both the Croix and Reims factories to the mid-1890s are presented in Table 5.1; Table 5.2 indicates their per annum rates of growth. (See also Appendix, Figure A.1). The two new factories received a boost on the closure of St Denis as they shared its redundant machinery and labour, though even before this their growth had been impressive, reaching an unprecedented average annual rate of 29 per cent at Croix between 1854 and 1861.[1] From the early 1850s to the late 1870s production showed a consistently upward trend. Subsequently, output was erratic, but indicated signs of rallying during the mid-1880s and again in the early 1890s. The rate of growth of output for the 30-year period 1854–84 averaged an astonishing 11.2 per cent at Croix and a remarkable 9.3 per cent at Reims. Even during the depressed 1880s, a positive growth was sustained.

Table 5.1: Production at Reims and Croix, 1850–94
(average annual output-kg)

	Reims	Croix
1850–54	331,047	227,293
1855–59	641,272	663,075
1860–64	–	1,812,833
1865–69	3,245,073	4,144,904
1870–74	3,516,377	5,411,791
1875–79	4,595,366	7,043,448
1880–84	4,745,005	6,267,680
1885–89	5,443,089	5,803,380
1890–94	4,541,241	6,040,834

Sources: L–I; L–VII/7, 10, 11; B–11A; B–13; B–61; B–69; B–71; B–79; G–1; G–2; By–1.

The extent of the Holden et fils empire is put into perspective by the figures presented in Table 5.3, which show the proportion of top used in the French worsted industry produced by the Croix and Reims

Table 5.2: Croix and Reims, annual rates of growth of output, selected periods, 1854–88

Croix	*%*	*Reims*	*%*
1854–61	29.0	1854–59	14.3
1854–84	11.2	1854–68	17.7
1861–68	12.5	1854–78	11.6
1861–78	8.5	1854–86	9.3
1861–88	5.0	1859–68	19.6
1868–78	5.8	1859–78	10.8
1868–88	2.5	1868–78	3.5
1871–78	8.9	1868–88	2.6
1880–88	1.0	1878–88	1.7
1881–88	2.6		

Source: as in Table 5.1.

factories. From the mid-1860s to the mid-1890s, the Holden enterprises produced 25 per cent of the industry's requirement of combed wool, with only a small fall during the depression of the late 1880s. During the last four decades of the nineteenth century, therefore, the Holden factories grew roughly in step with the French worsted industry as a whole.

Table 5.3: Market share of the Croix and Reims factories, 1851–94

	French consumption of combined wool (million kg)	*Total output Croix and Reims (million kg)*	*Market share %*
1851	10.6	.25	2.4
1855	12.4	1.64	13.2
1878	43.3	11.88	27.4
1894	46.7	10.76	23.0

Sources: The data were calculated from the following:
  1851: *Exposition* (1851), p. 138 and Table 5.1.
  1855: *Exposition* (1855); Table 5.1.
  1878: Alcan, *Fabrication des etoffes*, p. 456, Table 2. Picard, *Le Bilan*, p. 352 estimates worsted yarn production as 34 million kg = consumption of 35.4 million kg of combed wool giving Holden's market share as 33.6 per cent.
  1894: Grandgeorge, *Les Industries textiles* (1895), p. 70 and Table 5.1.

Because of the firm's practice of *autofinancement*, the rate of expansion was determined and constrained by the extent of retained capital. This was, despite the typically high profit levels, alternately frustratingly slow and aggravatingly fast for the partners.[2] During the early years of his tenure at Croix, Isaac Crothers regularly complained of the missed opportunities associated with the small size of his business. In 1857, for instance: 'if the mill was three times as large we should be kept working night and day';[3] 'if you agree to limit Croix to its present extent it will be a great loss.'[4] In subsequent years he reiterated the sentiment that expansion had been inadequate; but in 1868, Angus reported that 'both at Reims and Croix our extensions have been too rapid and both he [Isaac Crothers] and Jonathan have felt during last year that the production was ahead of the market instead of it being the reverse... it must be a lesson for the future".'[5]

By 1881, when the rate of return on capital was showing signs of weakening, and when the worsted trade generally was slack, Crothers, by then manager of both Reims and Croix, complained that

> our two extra card rooms have not only been no benefit, but they have been a heavy increase in wages...and all our other arrangements for 'production' have been burdens...for the future there will be no more additions of any kind not at Croix...there will be nothing more except a little at Reims.[6]

The policy and practice of commission combing clearly exacerbated the problems associated with expansion through *autofinancement*. Because the firm was dependent for its raw material upon the wool bought by its customers (the spinners) it had little, if any, control over supplies. Whilst the business was small, therefore, customers continually demanded faster work and the warehouses were full; whereas, following a period of expansion of the firm, the end of which coincided with a general slump: 'I am everyday harassed to know... where the wool is to come from to keep us going.'[7] The Croix plant was closed for two months in 1881, and short-time working was not unusual during the 1880s and 1890s; but generally, the system operated surprisingly smoothly.

While production and rates of growth of output were generally similar in the two factories, the underlying patterns of their success were quite different (See Table 5.4 and 5.5 below). In terms of productivity, for instance, Croix reached an early peak (in 1868) having performed very poorly from 1859 to 1862.[8] Although output per machine reached its maximum level in 1877 and subsequently declined rapidly, output per worker and total factor productivity fell consistently from 1868. Productivity performance at Reims exhibited a quite different pattern. In 1868, total factor productivity of Reims was only 0.87 that of Croix. In subsequent years, however, productivity gains were enormous, reaching a peak in 1886.[9] By 1890, total factor productivity of Reims exceeded that of Croix by more than 13 per cent.[10] The performance of the Croix mill was therefore more erratic and the figures suggest that the Reims factory was more solidly based

Isaac Holden et Fils – Croix 1863

and possibly more efficiently organised.[11] This was certainly the belief of Jonathan Holden when, in 1862, he requested a separation of the accounts; and from 1868 until he left the company, his Reims factory performed consistently better. Although the productivity of the Reims

Table 5.4: Croix and Reims, labour and machine comb productivity

	Croix			Reims	
	output/ worker per day (kg)	*output/ machine per day (kg)*		*output/ worker per day (kg)*	*output/ machine per day (kg)*
1856	7.0	—	1854	—	90.7
1859	9.0	—	1855	—	113.0
1861	7.6	—	1858	5.8	—
1868	11.5	153.5	1868	8.9	92.6
1877	9.6	157.5	1886	15.4	150.0
1884	10.6	123.0	1890	12.2	93.0
1886	10.1	97.0			
1890	10.4	80.4			

Source: as in Chapter 7, Tables 7.7, 7.8 and 7.9.

factory was sustained under Isaac Crothers' management to 1886, profit levels and return on capital exhibited immediate signs of weakening.[12]

Table 5.5: Croix and Reims, total factor productivity, [a]1868–90 (Selected periods)

Croix	Period	Total factor productivity
	1868:1877	0.91
	1868:1886	0.87
	1868:1890	0.93
Reims	1868:1890	1.17

Note:

a.   The calculations concern the joint productivity of labour and machine combs; the weights used for each factor are the respective shares of the total costs of production. Thus:

$$\frac{P_2}{P_1} = \left(\frac{Q_2/L_2}{Q_1/L_1}\right)^{S_L} \left(\frac{Q_2/K_2}{Q_1/K_1}\right)^{S_K}$$

where   P   is the joint productivity in period 1 and 2,
Q   is the total output in period 1 and 2,
L   is the labour force in period 1 and 2,
K   is the number of machine combs in period 1 and 2,
S_L is the average share of labour costs in total costs, and
S_K is the average depreciation of the machine combs used in the firms' calculation of total costs of production as a proportion of that cost.

Source: As in Table 5.4.

Table 5.6 and Appendix, Table A.1, which show the level of trading profits of the two factories and the percentage return on capital, demonstrate the capital-engendering capacity of the firms and thus the course of their sustained growth. Both firms achieved substantial returns on capital from an early stage, and each reached its peak of profit level and of percentage return on capital in the early 1870s. At Reims, in 1872, the rate of return on capital reached a staggering 55.6 per cent; and with the exception of 1867 and 1870, a figure of over 30 per cent was consistently recorded between 1863 and 1880.[13] Even during the depressed 1880s an average rate of 10 per cent was sustained, but negative figures were returned for the inclusive years 1892–94. In terms of profit, the Reims factory earned in the region of £1000 per week during the 1860s and £1500 per week in the 1870s. By the 1880s profits had reverted to the 1860s level, and by the 1890s losses were incurred. Between 1863 and 1880 over £1,000,000 of gross profit was earned at the Reims plant alone.

At Croix, while the return on capital never reached the heights of the Reims factory, the rates were still extraordinarily high and ranged from slightly under 20 per cent to rather more than 30 per cent from 1863 to

Table 5.6: Croix and Reims, rates of return on capital, 1860–94

Croix and Reims (total)

	Rate of return %	
1860	27.2	
1861	17.6	
1862	15.6	

	Croix Rate of return %	*Reims* Rate of return %
1863	22.9	38.3
1864	27.0	47.4
1865	23.0	48.6
1866	24.1	38.8
1867	15.3	26.9
1868	34.1	33.7
1869	34.0	34.7
1870	24.9	23.4
1871	29.1	32.2
1872	39.4	55.6
1873	35.5	46.9
1874	33.5	50.7
1875	25.5	36.6
1876	28.0	36.0
1877	30.0	41.6
1878	30.5	—
1879	25.8	—
1880	16.6	—
1881	9.8	7.9
1882	14.6	15.5
1883	13.4	14.7
1884	11.3	16.0
1885	2.5	7.9
1886	6.9	11.4
1887	1.9	9.2
1888	8.1	10.2
1889	—	—
1890	7.6	3.2
1891	5.7	3.1
1892	3.7	−0.35
1893	3.8	−0.64
1894	−1.3	−3.2

Source: as in Appendix, Table A.1.

1880 with a peak of 39.4 per cent in 1872.[14] Substantial fluctuations were experienced in the 1880s, from a peak in 1880 of 16.6 per cent to 1.9 per cent in 1887. Profit levels at Croix were generally poor before 1868 when profits were three times higher than in the previous year.[15] The improvement of the late 1860s was sustained throughout the 1870s when average weekly profit levels of £2,500 were achieved.[16] The general trading difficulties of the 1880s were reflected in erratic profits. Losses in 1885 and 1887 were preceded by profits of £6000 per month in the first four years of that decade. Profits rose towards the end of the 1880s before dropping again in the 1890s.

The figures presented in this chapter indicate that, while organised on the same principle and using identical machinery, the two Holden firms followed quite distinct courses and enjoyed contrasting fortunes. This suggests that they were exposed and responded to different external influences. The Reims concern expanded more slowly yet more consistently than Croix. The productivity figures support the view that while Reims employed an appropriate number of men and machines for the level of business, the Croix plant was over-capitalised much of the time. This may well reflect the nature of the local market, which was clearly more variable around Roubaix than in Reims, which comprised a stable spinning sector.[17] Isaac Crothers himself complained on more than one occasion that Roubaix corresponded in many ways to an American city, by which he meant that events were unpredictable and that planning was impossible. He summed up his perception of the distinction between the two cities in which his factories operated thus: 'At Reims they do wisely in taking their time there is no need to hurry...they have a regular trade the merino trade varying very little all the year round....Roubaix is more American and altogether different. It is either a great calm or a furious tempest.'[18] Certainly, the Croix factory was more prone to closures than was Reims and periodically had more work than it could handle. So, given the market situation in Roubaix/Croix which produced for a wider area than Reims, it was impossible for the firm to be run consistently at maximum efficiency.

The level of prices, and to a lesser extent the level of costs which influenced profits were likewise beyond the control of the individual firm. (see Table 5.7). At Croix, both costs and prices moved erratically. They fell – prices more rapidly than costs – to a minimum in 1860. During the 1860s both rose similarly leaving the differential unchanged. Costs at Croix fell from 1871 to 1878, then rose to 1880, whereafter they fluctuated but generally declined. Prices rose to 1877 and then fell continuously. From 1880 to 1892 the differential was very small, having been greatest during the 1850s when output was very small (see Appendix, Figure A.2). At the Reims factory the pattern was quite different (see Appendix, Figure A.3). Prices fell consistently yet

Isaac Holden et Fils – Reims 1863

less rapidly than at Croix and only rose slightly in the late 1880s. Costs followed no clear trend but generally moved inversely with prices. During the 1880s the cost/price differential was very small, and in 1881, as low as 1 centime. During the early 1890s, costs exceeded prices at both plants. By 1895, however, Angus Holden reported that 'our prospects are good... at Croix and Reims we have returned as far as to 55 centimes towards our old prices with success...all this looks more cheerful than we have experienced during the last five years.'[19] While prices are clearly outside the control of the entrepreneur, he can nevertheless influence some proportion of costs. At Croix, for instance, periodic overmanning resulted in both high labour costs and low worker productivity. While the effect of this on the differential may be very small, its impact on the profit level of a firm the size of Croix would be great.[20] At Reims, labour and machine inputs corresponded more consistently and economically to inputs of raw material and to desired output. Hence, costs were kept to a minimum and productivity gains were made until the late 1880s.[21]

While both the Holden concerns in France operated within different constraints, they each achieved a remarkable degree of success. Objective and subjective records indicate the ability of the Holden

Table 5.7: Croix, Reims and St Denis, unit prices and costs of combing (francs/kg of output), **1850–94**

	Croix		Reims		St Denis	
	Price	Cost	Price	Cost	Price	Cost
1850–54	1.54	0.67	1.63	0.68	—	—
1855–59	1.13	0.62	1.48	0.68	1.32	1.08
1860–64	0.89	—	—	—		
1865–69	1.07	0.81	1.13	0.82		
1870–74	1.23	0.84	1.17	0.79		
1875–79	1.10	0.83	1.04	0.68		
1880–84	0.80	0.70	0.77	0.66		
1885–89	0.61	0.66	0.64	0.58		
1890–94	0.61	0.73	0.60	0.74		

Source: as in Tables 5.1 and 5.2.

empire to combat effective competition and to transcend cyclical crises. The letters which flowed from the nephews to Isaac Holden provide a valuable insight into the organisation and operation of the firm, as well as the Holden family's perceptions of their position within the French woolcombing business. Successful commission combing required above all flexibility on the part of the comber. To maximise custom it was necessary to provide the facilities to comb all grades and thicknesses of wool. Holden had the advantage over competitors in owning a machine capable of processing a variety of wools.[22] The Holden partners clearly perceived the need to establish their positions within the industry before their own Square Motion and the other techniques that they controlled became generally available.

> We are commission combers and the top we make goes to all parts of France, but if combing machines are extensively sold we shall soon feel it with these large concerns... [but] by the time these machines fall into the public hands we shall be enabled to comb so cheap that few will take the trouble to mount them...[23]

Certainly Holden et fils was able to comb cheaply and even to drop prices in troubled times to retain custom: 'I have no doubt that it will be the best policy to make a concession to our spinning customers to prevent them from getting combing machines. As it is doubtful if they can comb as well as us consequently they will give us the preference.'[24] The quality of their combing, combined with their reliability and flexibility, secured for Holden et fils a large and growing market: 'They are well satisfied with our work and have decided to give us all their wool'.[25] 'Our customers here say that...we are the only combers who know how to deal with fine wools ... we are at the head of the trade for fine and intermediate wools ... [two manufacturers] have both declared the work to be the perfection of combing.' '...we have earned a famous reputation for making splendid top.'[26] Production figures and a consistent market share support the tenor of these statements.[27]

Successful commission combing further depended on the goodwill of custom and on a constant supply of raw wool. The latter was particularly difficult to ensure at Croix, and while at Reims customers kept the Holdens regularly supplied, the wool was of variable quality: 'we are full of wool... but mostly Buenos Ayres [sic]...therefore not at all for our district but quite [a] godsend and acceptable.[28] Holden's customers bought their raw wool at quarterly or monthly sales, and these purchases determined the pace of work during the succeeding weeks. Jonathan Holden and Isaac Crothers carefully scrutinised the sales activities and anticipated wool quantities: 'sales going off very well';[29] 'we have wool without end';[30] 'we may expect 30,000 bales from these sales';[31] 'our clients are doing very little at this stage...the prices are considered much too high for the price of merinos'.[32]

The strength of the Holden enterprise throughout the second half of the nineteenth century can be further indicated by their apparent superiority over immediate rivals and by their ability to contain the emergence of additional potential competitors: 'competitors are closing down'; 'top makers are continually disappearing'; 'our competitors are now fareing [sic] rather badly'; 'we shall go in and win it'; 'keep fine and intermediate to ourselves...Amédée and others will abandon them for more easy sorts not requiring so much care in combing'; 'we are... employed in all our fine rooms night and day... we have no reason to complain... our competitors are often standing here.'[33] During the early 1880s pressure on combing was great and many of the spinners with combing departments closed these down. In 1882, both Allart Rousseau and Morel offered their combing sections for sale to Holden.

The predominance of Holden et fils in the French worsted industry was attributed, by the family, to their possession of superior combing technology[34] which produced high-quality top; to their sensitivity to customers' requirements; and to their efficiency: 'it is efficiency that gives us a preference.'[35] It was not all plain sailing, however, though typically, the difficulties were surmounted with dexterity. Holden was pursued by patent disputes and litigation for much of his life, though he ultimately earned much from licence fees. The Square Motion continued to be a source of anxiety, and Holden was still patenting improvements to it in the late 1860s. This was at least partly to delay the time when his machine would become generally available. 'If there have been any improvements made in the combing machine lately, I shall be glad to see it.'[36] Thus the Holdens successfully minimised the distribution of the Square Motion, until it was too late to constitute a great threat.

Jonathan Holden's departure from Holden et fils was more than a minor irritation however, and for much of the 1880s the opposing Holden camps were locked in battle. Jonathan became involved with Harmel Frères, a company of Reims combers, who had developed a machine to remove burrs. Although the machine did not enjoy a good reputation ('it spoils the noils and does not free the top')[37], it bore a strong resemblance to a development of Holden's which typically he had failed to patent. Harmel and Jonathan Holden, who jointly owned the patent, began litigation, though Holden et fils were confident of winning and felt Harmel's demands for licence fees to be an insult.[38] Holden's machine, however, was found to be an infringement of Harmel's and he was forced to purchase the patents for £7500.

Jonathan's decampment was greatly resented by the Holden clan, but it seemed to inconvenience them only in the short term. Profits of the original Holden factory at Reims slumped in the year of the separation but quickly regained their former level, and, during the 1880s the 'Vieux Anglais' performed better than the Croix factory. For several years letters from Crothers to his uncle contained much invective against Jonathan – 'our competitor is maintaining his reputation as a third-class comber'[39] – and the letters suggest that Jonathan's factory was not enjoying success: 'by universal consent Jonathan's place [is] a failure... 'he of Reims has his machinery standing in daytime and he is evidently playing second fiddle.'[40] Although complete records of Jonathan Holden's business do not exist, data collected by the local prefecture show that at the turn of the century Jonathan was, in terms of machinery and labour employed, enjoying at least moderate success.[41]

Labour unrest troubled the Holden enterprises but only infrequently, and, it seems, to a lesser extent than other local manufacturers. In 1880, for instance, the workers at the Reims works struck for higher wages and a reduction in hours. This was granted almost immediately and the labour force returned to work. Two days later a general strike was called in the town which continued for some time, but Holden's work people did not participate. There is little suggestion, however, that Holden's industrial relations policy was significantly more enlightened than that of other manufacturers; and existing wage data indicate that Holden paid his workers only average rates, though these were negotiated with the workforce.[42]

Isaac Holden et fils, therefore, had no special or undeserved advantage over contemporary capitalists in the French worsted industry. They built up solid customer relationships and an enviable reputation in the trade. Holden had striven hard to develop a machine that would produce high-quality top. He then made strenuous attempts to restrict this superior machine for his own use. He acquired an awareness and an understanding of the operation of French woolcombing and he so organised his concerns as to adapt initially to existing conditions and then to influence their subsequent change to his own advantage. Once his position of predominance as a commission comber was established, it was virtually unchallengable, and it was the integrated combing concerns that were unable to withstand trade depression. Thus Holden had influenced the structure of the woolcombing business to suit his own requirements. It would be no exaggeration to state that throughout the second half of the nineteenth century, Holden stood at the centre of French woolcombing.

Notes

1   G–1
2   This was particularly true of Croix.
3   Isaac Crothers to Isaac Holden, 1 September 1867 (B–5B).
4   Isaac Crothers to Isaac Holden, 13 July 1857 (L–VII/8).
5   Angus Holden to Isaac Holden, 13 July 1868 (B–13); but this was at least partly in response to the trade crisis in 1867 which had been particularly pronounced in the Nord. See C. Fohlen, *L'Industrie textile au temps du second empire* (Paris, 1956), pp. 373–440.
6   Isaac Crothers to Isaac Holden, 14 January 1881 (G–2); and complaints of overproduction were common in the prefect's reports of the early 1880s: 'All commission combers have developed beyond the appropriate size and are now suffering the consequences of the exaggerated growth. It will be necessary for firms to go out of business or to reorganise themselves in order for an equilibrium to be reestablished' (*ADN*, 172M3).
7   Isaac Crothers to Isaac Holden, 18 January 1881 (G–2).
8   This had resulted in Jonathan requesting separate accounts (G–1).
9   Around 1880, Croix had more machines and almost twice as many workers whereas production was only slightly greater. Production in 1886 was 52 per cent greater than in 1868.
10   In 1886 it had been 25 per cent.
11   Its growth was certainly more measured and Angus may have been correct in his judgement that Croix was expanding too fast and was over-capitalised.
12   This may be explained by the establishment of Jonathan's competing factory which would doubtless have attracted some of the custom from the old factory.
13   The high points in 1872 illustrate the remarkable recovery from the Franco-Prussian War during which trade had been disrupted. 'Glory has cost us around a million', Isaac Crothers to Isaac Holden (27 July 1872, B–71).
14   The low point came in 1867 when return on capital was only 13.9 per cent. This was consistent with the experience of other manufacturers in the Nord. The crisis in the woollen and worsted industry was caused by the reopening of the cotton trade. The output of Amédée Prouvost's plant fell from 3.1 million kg in 1866 to 1.9 million kg in 1867 while profits fell from 89,452 francs (£3578) in 1866 to a loss of 192,696 francs (£7707) in 1867; and in the subsequent years Prouvost's instability was more pronounced than Holden's at Croix. See Fohlen, *L'Industrie textile*, pp. 337–400.
15   '...by far the best year we have ever had – the present year [1869] will be a brilliant year' Angus Holden to Isaac Holden, 30 June 1869 (B–13).

16 Croix had at least twice the assets of Reims.
17 Croix supplied a very much wider market, including many customers overseas. See also Chapter 7, p. 96.
18 Isaac Crothers to Isaac Holden, 5 May 1866 (L–VIII/7).
19 Angus Holden to Isaac Holden, 14 September 1895 (B–19).
20 For example, 1 centime per kg assuming 7 million kg output per year equal to £70,000, or £2,800 per fortnight.
21 Profits and return to capital were also maintained at a higher and more stable level at Reims than at Croix; and the cost/price differential was generally larger at Reims.
22 By 1858, the Croix plant had rooms for fine wools, coarse wools and still coarser wools. Isaac Crothers to Isaac Holden, 12 July 1858 (L–VII/9).
23 Jonathan Holden to Isaac Holden, January 1861 (L–VIII/2).
24 Isaac Crothers to Isaac Holden, 8 January 1883 (G–2).
25 Jonathan Holden to Isaac Holden, January 1861 (L–VIII/2).
26 Isaac Crothers to Isaac Holden, 7 April 1866 (L–VIII/7).
27 This remained at over 25 per cent from 1860 to 1900.
28 Jonathan Holden to Isaac Holden, 9 February 1877 (B–71).
29 Isaac Crothers to Isaac Holden, 4 May 1875 (B–15A).
30 Isaac Crothers to Isaac Holden, 26 April 1876 (B–15A).
31 Isaac Crothers to Isaac Holden, 9 May 1874 (G–2).
32 Jonathan Holden to Isaac Holden, 12 March 1875 (B–71).
33 Isaac Crothers to Isaac Holden, 29 December 1865 (L–VIII/6).
34 'With our new combs there is a future before us more brilliant than I have hitherto conceived.' Isaac Crothers to Isaac Holden, 14 July 1865 (L–VIII/6). '…the one we are making at Reims is much superior in every sense and very much cheaper with less liability to derangement.' Jonathan Holden to Isaac Holden, 12 July 1866 (B–5B).
35 Isaac Crothers to Isaac Holden, 14 January 1881 (G–2).
36 Jonathan Holden to Isaac Holden, 12 July 1866 (B–5B).
37 Isaac Crothers to Isaac Holden, 28 February 1883 (G–2).
38 'They are sure to lose their case.' Angus Holden to Isaac Holden, 22 July 1886 (B–17/18).
39 Isaac Crothers to Isaac Holden, 8 January 1883 (G–2).
40 *Ibid.*
41 In 1890, Jonathan Holden employed a labour force of 620 workers (*ADM*, 194M12). In 1902 this was 565 and at the same time Isaac Holden's factory employed 974 workers (*ADM*, 194M14). In 1904, Jonathan employed 72 machine combs while Isaac Holden employed 143. See Chapter 7, pp. 83–4, 89, for more details.
42 *ADM*, 194M9 and M11.

6 Isaac Holden et Fils: The Problems of Enterprise

It was at St Denis that Isaac Holden identified the type of factory organisation and operating principles that he subsequently replicated at Croix and Reims. He experimented with both technology and management until he was sure he had located the optimum arrangement. Thus it was during his tenure at St Denis that he was able to demonstrate, probably for the first time, his entrepreneurial skills.

His earlier entry into 'the anxious life of an employer of labour'[1] had ultimately failed, but it had, nevertheless, proved to be a valuable learning experience. He had suffered the inevitable years of trade depression, erratic demand, cash flow difficulties and the final blow of insolvency. It seems that Holden, overwhelmed by the desire to leave the employment of Townends, moved too quickly, with inadequate finance, and during a tenacious trade crisis, into independent enterprise. While the collapse of his small business was a profound disappointment, he had fared better than many of his competitors during the difficult economic climate of the 1840s. He had come unstuck because of the vagaries of the time and because of inadequate sources of borrowing, not through any personal or managerial weakness. Holden appreciated this and lost little confidence in his own entrepreneurial qualities and abilities.

A second chance for Holden to become his own boss occurred when he met Lister. The complementarity of the two men is referred to elsewhere; but clearly Holden needed Lister's capital to achieve his desired aim, while Lister required Holden's time and expertise to help him accumulate more capital. Holden used the opportunity presented by his partnership with Lister wisely. At St Denis he was able to experiment with both machinery and with management practices without, at first, having to worry too much about finance.

Even though Holden's attention was at least as much on technology as on manufacture, the business at St Denis expanded rapidly and profits averaged £2–3000 per month in the early 1850s.[2] Additional factories were built at Croix and Reims, where profit levels reached £10,000 per month during the 1860s and 1870s, and Holden family members joined the list of partners.[3]

The aim of this chapter is to elucidate the extent of Holden's success within the French worsted industry and to explore reasons for his achievement. While Isaac Crothers and Jonathan Holden played an integral part in the firm's success as the active managers of the Croix and Reims factories, Isaac Holden was by no means a sleeping partner. He continued to improve upon his Square Motion machine partly because additional patents kept it from competitors and partly because he truly desired to create a perfect machine. He spent much time either in France supervising the operations of his nephews or communicating instructions by frequent lengthy letters. Any change in practice or policy, however small, continued to require the endorsement of the founding partner.

Upon Lister's departure from the partnership in 1858, Holden's two sons were taken on as partners. The firm's title thus became Isaac Holden et fils and continued to be known as such until its closure.[4] Angus and Edward Holden, while based in Bradford, and actively involved in the factory there, made frequent visits to scrutinise the firm's operations at Croix and Reims.

The relationship between Isaac Crothers and Jonathan Holden on the one hand and the Holden brothers on the other was clearly tinged with suspicion and mistrust. While Isaac Holden's disarming approach to the difficulties this caused eased the situation in the short term, ultimately, familial rivalry proved terminal. In 1860, before he wound up St Denis, Holden proposed to reward his nephews for their efforts by offering them a managing partnership in the firm. His sons resented the implications of this step, and Angus attempted to persuade his father not to proceed:

> What need have we to sell shares in one of the best businesses in existence on such easy terms, to, I don't care who?...But I think we are not at all warranted in selling a fifth or any share each to Jonathan and Isaac on such terms as you proposed and they can have no conceivable right to expect it... for my sake don't let us have any more partners...allow them a percentage of the profit.'[5]

This plea failed to move Isaac, and by mid-1860, Jonathan Holden and Isaac Crothers each acquired a 10 per cent share of the business.[6]

Family conflict subsequently worsened and eventually took the form of animosity between the two nephews. In 1863, Jonathan Holden requested an alteration to the firm's accounting procedure, which, until then, had amalgamated the books of Croix and Reims. Jonathan believed that a separation of the accounts would reveal his own superior achievement and Isaac Crothers' underhand dealings:

> Isaac has [been] overdrawing his stipulated allowance and is guilty of gros [sic] negligence, indifference and mismanagement and finally ruining a good business in which he might have made millions...the entire business has made f. 2,731,407.98 [c. £110,000] since Jan. 1859 of which Reims has

contributed f. 2,267,288.15 consequently Croix f. 464,119,83 during which time Isaac has drawn f. 85,404…I demand a devolution.[7]

Isaac Holden took these accusations and requests seriously and dispatched his sons to investigate. The performance of each factory was systematically tested during 1864, but no significant differences between them were apparent: '…the results are very much the same…Croix has made a little more top…[each machine] could comb 100 kilo per day.'[8] Isaac Holden again revealed his disarming qualities when, despite the lack of evidence to support Jonathan's case, he nevertheless agreed to the restructuring of the nephews' shares so that each was given a one-fifth part of that mill for which he was responsible. Although Holden intended that this should placate Jonathan, the separation of interest, which allowed the progress of each firm to be charted individually, backfired on Jonathan. By 1868, it was patently clear that Jonathan's performance was overshadowed by that of Isaac Crothers: 'Croix made more than Reims so that Isaac has rather cut out Jonathan this time, this proves what can be done with good fine wools and good machinery.'[9] In fact, Croix achieved a significantly higher rate of productivity – 56,012 kg per machine per annum – compared with an output at Reims of 33,802 kg per machine per annum.[10]

Understandably, Jonathan was enraged by these findings. By the early 1870s, his petulant behaviour resulted in a formalisation and extension of the accounting separation. The partnership deed of 1872 recognised distinct controlling groups at Croix and Reims. As a result of this, Jonathan Holden was to drop an interest in the Croix plant and to commit himself entirely to the Reims business, while Isaac Crothers was to be engaged only in Croix. Isaac, Angus and Edward Holden constituted the remaining partners at each location.[11]

While the outcome was precisely what Jonathan had originally desired, he interpreted the action as family conspiracy. Relationships with his cousins and uncle continued to deteriorate and he failed to 'make up his mind and be content and delighted with what he had'.[12] Throughout the 1870s, Jonathan complained incessantly to Holden about Crothers, to the latter's irritation.[13] Jonathan felt himself to be a victim of vituperation and believed Crothers to be acting contrary to previous agreements;[14] while Crothers, for his part, stated that Jonathan 'exacerbated the situation by reneging on agreements made among the parties'.[15] While it is unclear which of the two was more at fault, Jonathan was the more volatile and emotional in his response to this and subsequent difficulties. He frequently accused Crothers of obsequiousness, and Isaac Holden of partisanship and of having 'widened the breech'.[16] By the late 1870s, it had become obvious to all

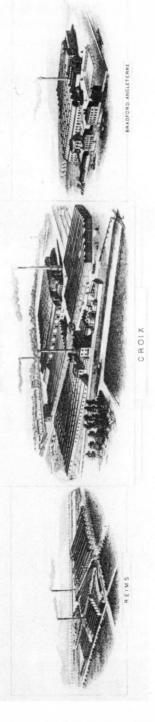

Letterhead of Isaac Holden and Sons, c. 1870

Isaac Holden, 1885

Issac Holden Crothers   Thomas Craig
Angus Holden   Issac Holden   Edward Holden,   c. 1882

The Holden Comb, Bradford Industrial Museum

Samuel Cunliffe Lister, 1875

Jonathon Holden

that Jonathan's position was untenable, and, in 1880, when all attempts to heal the rift had failed, Jonathan resigned his partnership in Isaac Holden et fils, and immediately established a competing mill in Reims.

Accordingly, later in 1880, a new partnership agreement was drawn up among the remaining four family members. Isaac Crothers became manager of both the Croix and the original Reims factory, which became known as the 'Vieux Anglais'.[17] Jonathan, meanwhile, forged ahead with his 'Nouvel Anglais'. His desire for independence stemmed largely from the resentment he felt towards his family, both for their limited appreciation of his efforts and performance and for their conspiracy against him. The height of his antagonism (1875–80) coincided with the period when many Reims worsted spinning mills were shutting down their combing sections, and being replaced by specialist combers.[18] Jonathan believed not only that the market for commission combing was expanding but that he enjoyed a strong personal following in the locality which would ensure him a steady trade. Although there remain few data about the course of Jonathan's rival factory, it seems that, contrary to the hopes and expectations of his family, he was successful.[19] He became a benefactor of the town of Reims, a public library featuring among his donations;[20] a street named after him remains to this day.

Despite the potentially destructive nature of Jonathan's actions, the 'Vieux Anglais' continued to prosper along with the Croix branch of Isaac Holden et fils. No further internecine rivalry occurred following Jonathan's departure, and the composition of the partnership remained unchanged from then until Isaac Holden's death in 1897. The *patron*, however, contemplated a restructuring of the firm to take effect from the moment of his demise. His idea was to establish a *société en commandite*[21] to allow for the admittance of sleeping partners. This was believed to be the best course of action as *commandites* in France were 'as common as two penny pies'. Isaac was anxious to secure the relevant deeds before his death, while his son Angus, with responsibility for clarifying the arrangement, saw no need to hurry: 'Whether it is done *voluntarily before* the death of the deceased partner, or compulsorily after his death does not matter.'[22]

Nevertheless, in 1896, the *commandite* deed was drawn up, allowing for heirs and representatives of the demised partners, known as *commanditaires*, to receive remuneration from the business.[23] Following Isaac Holden's death in 1897, Angus Holden and Isaac Crothers became sole managing partners in the firm, and these two, together with Edward Holden, were named *commanditaires*. Isaac Holden's shares (6/16th) were equally distributed among the *commanditaires* as were any subsequent profits.[24] By this agreement, therefore, Isaac Holden et fils became, in principle, semi-public, though in practice it remained in the family for many more years.

As earlier chapters have shown, Holden's commercial success in France was exceptional. It brought him not only material wealth but also great prestige and respect as an entrepreneur. He became established as a leading member of the textile authority in France. He was the recipient of numerous medals and prizes for exhibits of his machines and products.[25] His knowledge of both the English and French worsted industry was revered and he was frequently called upon to give evidence to French committees of inquiry.[26]

While Holden was by no means a self-made man, he clearly perceived himself as such. He certainly practised many of the well-rehearsed Victorian virtues, and he attributed his success to hard work, energy, efficiency, self-education, thrift and deferred gratification.[27] It is unlikely, however, that a long-term, successful entrepreneur would be devoid of these values, and while Holden may have utilised them to an exceptional degree, this fact alone is insufficient to explain his extraordinary success.

There is no doubt that Holden overcame the day-to-day problems typical of running a business with efficiency and that he turned many potential difficulties to his advantage. His ability to remain calm in the face of internecine familial rivalry has been discussed. Even more significant, perhaps, was his attitude towards labour unrest. He appreciated very early in his entrepreneurial career the damage an unruly workforce might cause. He was led to believe that French workers were in many ways inferior to the English, and he therefore recruited only English workers to positions of influence within the firm (recall that he also did this to ensure loyalty).[28] Whether or not his assessment of the relative strengths of French and English labour was accurate, or even justified, it is clear that the key workers in his business were dedicated and eminently trustworthy.

Holden became a characteristically French paternalist employer and this apparently suited his nature.[29] From the start of the business in St Denis, he established a mill community. He provided housing for his workforce and built a nonconformist chapel which his employees were expected to attend.[30] He was explicitly interested in the 'welfare' of his workers, though the manner in which he influenced their working and living environments clearly operated to his own advantage.[31] Holden repeated the community ideal at the Croix and Reims factories – indeed at Croix, the mill and its associated community shaped the subsequent growth of the town to the extent that even today it is referred to as 'Holden City'.[32]

There is no doubt that Holden's workforce were comparatively compliant. The incidence of strikes at the Croix and Reims factories was considerably less than at others in the locality. Unrest generally was muted and rapidly terminated; and negotiations over wages and other aspects of working conditions were quickly completed.[33] Holden himself believed that his healthy labour relations record was the result of above-average wage levels and attractive working and living conditions. While there is little evidence to support either of these statements, his paternalistic, even autocratic style of management clearly extracted obedience and commitment from his workforce.

Problems of capital acquisition and cash flow which had defeated Holden in his early capitalist efforts rarely existed in his partnership with Lister or subsequently. Initially, Lister had provided much of the necessary capital, both for equipping the business and for purchasing patents. Expansion of the firm at St Denis, and the building of the Croix and Reims factories, was financed largely from retained profits. The risk of cash-flow difficulties was minimised by the principle upon which the work process operated – that of commission combing. Thus, circulating capital constituted a very minor component of total capital needs, and once the factories were established, capital was necessary only to finance replacement machinery or an expansion programme. Profit levels were directly influenced by the vagaries of major customers, but even in times of severe trade depression, the Holden enterprises were able to remain on an even keel as firms around them collapsed. Commission combing, therefore, significantly minimised the degree of risk involved in worsted manufacturing in the second half of the nineteenth century.

Holden was thus organisationally canny and efficient, but he was especially distinguished from potentially similar entrepreneurs of the time by his technological interest and expertise. It was a fascination in woolcombing technology that had drawn him and his partner, Lister, together. It was because of Lister's financing that Holden was able to continue to develop his machine and to experiment with working practices in the early years at St Denis. And it was because of Lister's desire to obtain – and willingness to purchase – competing patents that Holden, on breaking the partnership with Lister, found himself in a monopoly position with respect to woolcombing technology. This enabled him to restrict the extent of the technology that was available to competitors and to confine, for many years, the use of the Square Motion machine to his own factories. Despite Lister's critical role as financier, it was Holden who appreciated the value of efficient woolcombing technology generally, and the worth of his own Square Motion machine in particular. He clearly understood that the essence of factory combing lay in a combination of superb machinery and efficient, faultless organisation, and it is in this perception that the key to Holden's entrepreneurial greatness must lie.

While Holden's personal qualities were clearly conducive to success in business, the way in which the workers and work process were organised around a particularly suitable machine largely explains the extraordinary performance of Isaac Holden et fils. Holden's brand of entrepreneurship typified the French businessman and suited him well. The practice of commission combing was known in France before Holden's arrival, but it was he who exploited its full potential. Holden thought carefully about the system, particularly in terms of its relationship with his Square Motion machine, which, because of its size, necessitated large-scale production. Indeed the Square Motion machine was ideally suited to the type of production that Holden established. Because he had considered commission combing as a principle as well as in its practical application, its effectiveness for Holden was naturally greater than for those for whom commission combing was merely a response to economic circumstances.

It has been stated earlier in this study that Holden believed his success in commission combing lay in his organisational abilities and his complete reliability which was of critical importance for the customers. Although a self-confessed virtue, the confidence of his customers was apparent in the growth and stability of the firm. Other, less committed combers attracted less steady custom and were consequently the first to collapse in periods of economic depression. Holden gradually attracted custom away from his competitors until not only had he attained a near monopoly as a commission comber, but had also forced the closure of many combing sections of spinning factories.

It seems, therefore, that Isaac Holden succeeded in the long term because he was a hardworking, skilful businessman; because he conformed easily to the pattern of the typical French entrepreneur; and because he was an able and persistent inventor and technician. He clearly enjoyed good fortune and the impact of his partnership with Lister on his future should not be underestimated. He never took his success for granted, however, and tackled setbacks with equanimity.

Emphasis so far has been placed upon the critical developments in the early stages of the mechanisation of woolcombing and on Holden's achievements in his extensive manufacturing empire. The influence Holden exerted on the entire structure of woolcombing in France during the second half of the nineteenth century remains to be analysed. The next chapter, therefore, places Holden's activities within the context of the French woolcombing industry. It also makes an assessment of the extent to which his patenting and other protective activities affected the general diffusion of woolcombing technology. Finally the organisation of woolcombing production is examined, in terms of its relationship with both Holden's manufacturing activities and with the technical choices available to the industry in general.

Notes

1 Quoted in E. Jennings, 'Sir Isaac Holden (1807–1897): "The First Comber in Europe"' (Ph.D, University of Bradford, 1982), p. 332.
2 L–VII/7.
3 G–1.
4 See partnership agreements in B–85.
5 Angus Holden to Isaac Holden, 14 February 1860 (L–VIII/1).
6 Angus and Edward each had a 20 per cent share and Isaac 40 per cent. The two managing partners corresponded regularly with each other and with Isaac Holden.
7 Jonathan Holden to Isaac Holden, 3 December 1863 (B–12).
8 Angus Holden to Isaac Holden, 17 September 1864 (B–11A).
9 Angus Holden to Isaac Holden, 30 June 1869 (B–13).
10 Calculated from information in *ibid.*
11 Partnership deed 1872 (B–85).
12 Angus Holden to Isaac Holden, 29 June 1871 (B–71).
13 '...mainly [because of] Jonathan's manner of never speaking or writing to *me* but continually harassing you and Edward and Angus with *petits comptes* against me.' Isaac Crothers to Isaac Holden, 30 April 1875 (B–71).
14 Jonathan Holden to Isaac Holden, 4 February 1875 (B–71).
15 Isaac Crothers to Isaac Holden, 30 April 1875 (B–71).
16 Jonathan Holden to Isaac Holden, 11 February 1875 (B–71) and 6 March 1875 *ibid.*, where he accuses Isaac Holden of taking Crothers' side: 'you want to trip me up from behind'. To Crothers he wrote, 'Now be advised from a friend not to play such paltry tricks...he will consider you a mere sycophant.' 17 March 1875 (B–71).
17 Partnership agreement 1880 (B–82).
18 Letters written in 1875 and 1876, (B–71).
19 Isaac Crothers to Isaac Holden, 8 January 1883 (G–2). He made references to 'this third-class comber'.
20 '...a crafty bid of popularity worthy of its author'. Angus Holden to Isaac Holden, 26 July 1887 (B–17/18).
21 Its nearest equivalent was a limited liability company.
22 Angus Holden to Isaac Holden, 8 February 1896 (B–19).
23 *Commanditaires* could demand the dissolution of the partnership if the managing partners did not perform their functions properly.
24 Partnership agreement 1896 (By–1).
25 A full list of these is to be found in Jennings, 'Sir Isaac Holden', pp. 340–1.
26 He was also called upon to give evidence to the Select Committee on Letters Patent set up by the British House of Commons in 1871. In 1860, he appeared before the Chevalier Committee on the Anglo-French Commercial Treaty. Holden's testimony appears in *Enquête industrielle sur le traité de commerce avec l'Angleterre* (Paris, 1860), vol. 3, pp. 479–89.
27 See Jennings, 'Sir Isaac Holden', pp. 331–2.
28 *Ibid.*, p. 336.
29 For recent work on the character of the French entrepreneur and entrepreneurship, see L. Bergeron, *Les Capitalistes en France, 1780–1914* (Paris, 1978); C. Fohlen, 'Entrepreneurship and Management in France in the Nineteenth Century', in P. Mathias and M. M. Postan (eds), *The Cambridge Economic History of Europe*, vol. VII, Part 1 (Cambridge, 1978), pp. 347–81. For a specific case study of a Roubaisien textile family, and the general issue of French business, see D. Landes, 'Religion and Enterprise: The Case of the French Textile Industry'; and M. Lévy-Leboyer, 'Innovation and Business Strategies in Nineteenth and Twentieth-century France', in E. C. Carter, R. Forster, and J. N. Moody, *Enterprise and*

Entrepreneurs in Nineteenth and Twentieth-Century France (London, 1976), pp. 41–86, pp. 87–135, respectively.

30 See Jennings, 'Sir Isaac Holden', p. 337.
31 *Ibid.*, p. 336.
32 Jean Piat, *Croix: Dix siècles d'histoire* (Croix, 1972), Chapter 6.
33 Much of the context of the following paragraphs is dealt with at greater length in earlier chapters.

There is no doubt that the direction of technical change within the woolcombing industry and the distribution of woolcombing technology in France was largely dictated by Holden's patenting activities. The numerous and often highly intricate battles over patent rights which so occupied Lister and Holden during the 1850s directly influenced the nature of subsequent inventive effort and the extent to which the products of this were diffused. When Isaac Holden purchased his partner's share of the business, he inherited an impressive portfolio of patents. Appearing before the Chevalier Committee on the Anglo-French treaty in 1860, Holden claimed ownership of 45 woolcombing patents, 17 of which had originally belonged to other patentees.[1] It is impossible to determine how many of these patents were for new machines, but it is known that from them only three machine combs materialised that were used extensively in the French worsted industry in the second half of the nineteenth century – the Heilmann, the Square Motion and the Noble machine comb.

Holden had direct control over the Square Motion and Noble machine comb, and for a short time also the Heilmann machine comb, and this influence severely limited the extent and the content of the diffusion of woolcombing technology. Holden's powerful position also benefited the performance of his own enterprises, and for many years, his competitors were disadvantaged as he kept the most appropriate technology out of their reach. At the same time, with the aid of patents for non-marketable machines in his possession, Holden perfected his own machinery which allowed his system of combing to become the organising principle of the woolcombing industry.

The organisation of woolcombing production – particularly the emergence of woolcombing as a separate industry within worsted production – can be seen at least partly as the result of Holden's manipulation of the evolving patent system and his influence as a practising comber. Holden's enviable position with respect to patent control lasted for twenty years from 1850, during which time he assured his enduring position within the industry. Indeed, the long-term pattern of the industry's organisation was established between 1850 and 1870 with Holden at the centre. Although many of the original patents expired after 1870, and the machinery based upon them, including the Square Motion and Noble machine comb, became more freely available, Holden's position was not challenged. So although 1870 marked a watershed in the competitive environment, and although the profitability of the Reims and Croix factories reflected this change, output remained at unprecedented high levels. Holden therefore ensured that the technical and organisational structure of his firms not only permitted their own longevity but also influenced the nature and extent of their competition.

The technical achievements of the second half of the nineteenth century dictated changes in the scale and structure of woolcombing production. These developments took place in two stages corresponding to the broad outlines of the diffusion of woolcombing technology. An expansion in the scale of enterprise occurred generally between 1850 and 1870 as more Heilmann machine combs became employed in the worsted industry. There was little consistency in structure, however, and as the market grew rapidly after 1850, a variety of organisational forms developed in diverse locations. Worsted spinners, as well as specialist combers, produced combed wool in the major worsted centres of northern France – Reims, Fourmies, Roubaix and Tourcoing.

This diffuse structure was eroded after 1870, however, by the generally depressed conditions in the industry (taking its toll of small producers) and by the greater availability of the Square Motion and Noble machine combs. The combination of these features ultimately led to a strengthening of the position of the specialist combing concerns. The scale of the woolcombing enterprises grew at an unprecedented rate and this sector of the industry became the most capital-intensive and the most labour-intensive. Worsted spinners in Reims and Fourmies who had previously combed sufficient wool for their own purposes closed their combing plants and relinquished the work to the specialist combers of northern France. By the end of the nineteenth century, these combers processed the bulk of the raw wool consumed by French worsted manufacturers. They were few in number and all operated within immense units which were organised on the principles pioneered by Holden.

In the years before 1870, the Heilmann comb was the most popular means of combing wool mechanically in France. As soon as Nicolas Schlumberger had made Heilmann's machine comb operational and had begun to construct it in his Guebwiller factory, it proved a great success among worsted manufacturers. One of the first purchasers of the Heilmann machine comb was Paturle-Lupin of Le Cateau, who had the machine installed in 1850. Within a year, two neighbouring firms had installed eleven Heilmann combs; and also in 1851, the extensive woollen and worsted company of Lefebvre-Ducatteau in Roubaix began to use the machine.[2] Their confidence in the new technology was further demonstrated when they engaged Amédée Prouvost (Lefebvre's brother-in-law) to establish the region's first specialist combing concern employing exclusively the Heilmann machine.[3] In Reims, as in the Nord, worsted spinners were quick to exploit the new technology.[4]

Heilmann's machine comb was an immense technical achievement, and was clearly recognised as such. The French commissioners to the Great Exhibition of 1851 did not hesitate to extol its virtues, and French worsted spinners gave it their unreserved support.[5] According to Isaac Holden's own notes, 275 Heilmann machine combs were working in France as early as 1856. Table 7.1 illustrates their geographical distribution and indicates that the Heilmann machine comb was employed in those worsted areas which had emerged in the decade before the mechanisation of combing, and less in those areas of France traditionally associated with handcombing. After only six years on the market, therefore, more than two-thirds of the Heilmann machine combs were working outside the previous strongholds of handcombing.

Table 7.1: Distribution of Heilmann machine combs, 1856

	Number	%
Fourmies-Le Cateau	100	36
Roubaix	60	22
Alsace	55	20
Reims	20	7
Tourcoing	20	7
Other	20	7

Source: B–91/8

Over the following ten years, the demand for the Heilmann machine comb was sustained at a high rate; and in 1867, according to J. E. Charles Seydoux in a report to the International Jury of the Paris Universal Exhibition of that year, a total of 1200 machines were installed in French enterprises.[6] In the intervening years, judging by the information presented in Table 7.2, Reims had emerged as a major centre of woolcombing, and together with Fourmies-Le Cateau and Roubaix, accounted for 89 per cent of the country's combing capacity.

The information in Tables 7.1 and 7.2 suggests that the new woolcombing technology, despite its general availability had a particular pattern of ownership. In the first decade of its use, organisational differences were reflected in the scope of adoption of the Heilmann machine comb.

In and around Reims, for instance, a large and established handcombing sector existed, but no interest in machine combing was

Table 7.2: Distribution of Heilmann machine combs, 1867

	Number	%
Fourmies-Le Cateau[1]	331	28
Reims[2]	440	37
Roubaix[3]	282	24
Tourcoing[4]	100	7
Other[5]	47	4
Total	1200	100

Sources:
1. A. Falleur, *Fourmies*, p. 26.
2. *Exposition Universelle de 1867*, p. 110.
3. *Ibid.*
4. Estimated from *ADN*, M653/28–34 and A. Goblet, *Le Peignage de la laine à Roubaix-Tourcoing et son évolution économique et sociale*, (Lille, 1903), p. 72.
5. *Exposition Universelle de 1867*, p. 108.

shown by the master combers.[7] Consequently, the worsted spinners extended their mills to include combing, adopted the new technology, and thus displaced the master comber and his workforce.[8] As a result, the typical organisation of woolcombing in Reims became the integrated spinning and combing mill. Before Lister and Holden built their factory in Reims in 1852, there were already 63 machine combs operating in integrated mills.[9] Theirs was the only specialist combing factory that survived the second half of the nineteenth century, and at no time during this period were there more than three such concerns.[10]

The organisation of woolcombing production that emerged in Fourmies, was not unlike the Reims pattern. Before combing was successfully mechanised, the worsted spinners of Fourmies typically employed handcombers who worked from their own homes. As soon as Heilmann's machine comb was proved to be commercially viable, these spinners simply replaced their handcombers with the new machinery. As in Reims, the spinning mills were extended to include combing on the premises. Once begun, this process of transformation was rapidly completed. By 1852, there were seven integrated spinning and combing mills in Fourmies, employing a total of 42 Heilmann machine combs.[11] Over the next six years, eight more integrated mills were established, and in the biggest push between 1863 and 1867, 15 such mills were set up.[12] In 1870, at the end of this expansionary period, the worsted spinners of Fourmies were employing about 200 machine combs for their own use.[13] Some spinners in Fourmies, however, did not produce their own combed wool. Their numbers are unknown, but in 1859, it was reported that five specialist combing concerns were working on commission in Fourmies.[14] With an average of only 20 workers each, the capacity of these specialist concerns was small compared to both the integrated mills in Fourmies and the specialist combing enterprises found in Reims, Roubaix and Tourcoing at the same time.[15] Later evidence suggests, however, that unlike the situation in Reims, specialist combing concerns grew faster than combing within integrated mills in Fourmies. In 1870, for example, there were only five specialist combing concerns in the town; but they were far larger than their earlier counterparts and employed about 20 per cent of the total number of machine combs in the region.[16]

While Fourmies and Reims shared similar characteristics in their organisation of woolcombing production, Roubaix and Tourcoing each exhibited a distinct pattern. Tourcoing had been the principal centre of handcombing in France, and here, as in other traditional handcombing areas, the mechanisation of woolcombing proceeded slowly. Whereas handcombing had largely been displaced from the other major worsted-producing areas within a few years of the Heilmann machine comb becoming available, handcombing persisted in Tourcoing until 1868.[17] The adoption of mechanised techniques did not fundamentally alter the organisation of production; the master comber and his workforce were replaced by the specialist combing factory and its operatives.[18]

In Roubaix, however, where there was no tradition of handcombing, the appearance of the machine comb resulted in the establishment of a new industrial activity. Before the opening of two specialist combing concerns – Allart Rousseau in 1846, and Dujardin-Collet in 1847[19] – Roubaix had relied entirely on Tourcoing for its supply of combed wool. In 1853, when production began at Lister and Holden's factory in Croix, Isaac Holden noted that there were already five specialist combing concerns in Roubaix.[20] The largest of these, Dujardin-Collet was producing 1200 kg of combed wool daily on their own patented machine combs;[21] while the combing enterprises of Amédée Prouvost and Jules Delarue, employing the Heilmann and Collier machine combs respectively, each produced 600 kg of combed wool per day.[22] The other two combers, Allart Rousseau and Louis Cordonnier, both used Heilmann's machine comb and produced, respectively, 400 and 50 kg per day.[23] Thus by the mid-1850s, the output of combed wool from Roubaix's specialist combing plants exceeded the total output of Tourcoing's hand and machine combing sector.[24]

Heilmann had conceived the machine comb in relation to cotton production. Both his collaborator, J.B. Bourcart, and his patron, Nicolas Schlumberger, were involved in cotton, the former as an engineer and the latter as a substantial industrialist.[25] The problem of combing was solved in the context of spinning, so the machine was originally intended to complement cotton-spinning technology. When, several years later, the machine comb was modified to process wool, it was similarly intended as a complement to spinning. It is not surprising, therefore, that the earliest and most receptive exponents of Heilmann's technology in the worsted industry were the spinners of Fourmies-Le Cateau, Alsace and Reims. In fact, the Heilmann machine comb was particularly well-suited to the needs of these spinners, as it performed best with the fine, short, merino wool on which their production was based.[26] The smallness of the Heilmann machine comb was also an attractive feature. Its output was 20–25 per cent that of the larger Square Motion and Noble machine combs,[27] which suited the majority of French worsted spinners who did not possess sufficient individual spinning capacity to absorb the output of even one of these larger machines.[28] In other words, where integrated spinning and combing mills predominated, the Heilmann machine comb was the more appropriate and popular technology.

The technical requirements of the specialist combers, however, were quite different from those of the spinners. In many cases, the varied needs of their customers required them to comb a wide range of staple lengths efficiently; and typically, their scale of operation was much larger than the combing sections of integrated mills. The Heilmann machine comb was thus unsatisfactory for their purposes; and the most appropriate technology – the Square Motion and the Noble machine combs – was not generally available until the 1870s. Holden had an advantage over other specialist combers because of his control of these techniques.

In the first few years of its existence, the Square Motion was effectively hidden from the industry by secrecy; and subsequently, the basic design and modifications were protected by patent. For at least 20 years, therefore, Holden was guaranteed sole rights as user and constructor of the machine. Holden's patent purchasing activities suppressed many other designs, and allowed some to be incorporated, wholly or partly, into the Square Motion's improvements.[29] Despite several attempts to make and market illegal copies, the Square Motion remained strictly confined to Holden's factories until the 1870s. The circulation of the Noble machine comb was also limited. Holden had become the licensee of this machine under the terms of the purchase of the Noble patent;[30] and while there were no restrictions on the number that could be produced, prospective purchasers were faced with a licence fee of 20,000 francs.[31] This sum was equivalent to the profit made from running the machine comb for two and a half years (at current prices and costs) and was therefore sufficient to deter all but the most determined or confident combers.[32]

Thus, by various means, Holden forced other specialist combers to accept what was, for their purposes, a second-best technology. For at least 20 years, Holden was one of the few combers in France equipped with the most appropriate and efficient technology of the time. As for the Heilmann technology employed in the integrated spinning and combing mills in Reims and Fourmies, Holden had little control over its diffusion, except between 1858 and 1861 when he was its licensee.[33]

Holden's major problem, therefore, seemed to be the competition of the integrated concerns. In Reims, for instance, stringent attempts were made to deter the spinners from doing their own combing, as reflected in much of the communication between Jonathan Holden in Reims and Isaac Crothers in Croix, and Isaac Holden in Bradford. An early letter, dated 14 April 1860, outlines this strategy succinctly:[34]

> My opinion is that we should prevent by a timely reduction of our prices, any of our customers from mounting combing, which we can do without doubt, for even when we reduce to what is considered their best price of f. 0.90, it will leave us in good profit...the difficulty with me and my opinion is to know the real intentions of our customers and to keep up the price as long as possible and still by timely reductions insure ourselves of their work. There is a strong feeling amongst them at present, that in order to make business profitable, they must do all themselves or they will be run down by English competition.

Until the 1870s, however, their strategy met with little success. Although Jonathan was able to offer consistently falling commission prices to his customers – indeed, prices fell by as much as 50 per cent between 1854 and 1875[35] – the number of machine combs employed in the worsted industry increased dramatically.

Table 7.3: Machine combs in Reims worsted industry, 1853–1903

Year	Number
1853	63
1858	246
1861	350
1878	709
1903	237

Sources: 1853: D. M. Gordon, 'Merchants and Capitalists', p. 117.
1858; 1861: *ADM*, 172M3.
1878: *Chambre de Commerce de Reims*, p. 19.
1903: E. Lefèvre, *Histoire économique*, p. 231.

Jonathan's hopes of reducing the amount of competition in Reims did not begin to materialise until the late 1870s. The boom in combing, evident from the early 1850s, showed signs of waning towards the end of the 1860s, and several prominent spinning mills were forced to abandon combing operations established in response to the sudden increase in demand for worsteds which had emerged during the cotton famine of the mid-1860s.[36] After 1875, however, judging from the accounts of the Reims factory, general economic conditions became desperate. Prices fell precipitously and, while before 1886 the stable costs squeezed profit margins, after 1886 profit margins plummeted as costs rose. From 1886 to 1895 the consistent losses at the Holden factory[37] were absorbed by the enormous profits which the factory had previously made and output continued at high levels.[38] Other factories, however, were less fortunate, and between 1875 and 1900 a progressive decline in combing capacity took place. Another 14 integrated mills closed their combing operations and reverted to spinning; and a total of 239 machine combs were withdrawn from the industry.[39] Only three enterprises producing combed wool remained in Reims at the end of the century – those of Isaac Holden, Jonathan Holden, and the smaller firm of L. and H. Collet. These factories with a total of 237 machine combs (mostly Square Motions) between them in 1904 more than adequately satisfied the demand for combed wool from the city's worsted spinners whose production capacity had changed little over the previous 30 years.[40]

Until the 1880s, Fourmies was probably the nearest rival to Reims in terms of woolcombing capacity. Isaac Holden never owned a plant there, though he was indirectly associated with the establishment of one factory, and clearly influenced the organisation of the woolcombing sector of the town. Judging from the data on the number of machine combs presented in Table 7.4, the growth of woolcombing was as dramatic in Fourmies as in Reims. Capacity increased more than 15 times between 1853 and its maximum level in 1889. The upward trend continued for longer than in Reims, but contraction in the late nineteenth century was common to both cities.

While the total number of machine combs grew to the 1890s, the number of machine combs in integrated mills began to fall relatively

Table 7.4: Machine combs in Fourmies, 1853–1910

Year	Number
1853[1]	42
1859[2]	143
1867[1]	335
1878[1]	520
1885[3]	646
1897[4]	418
1910[5]	108

Sources: 1. *A. Falleur, Fourmies*, p. 26.
2. *ADN*, M653/27; *Enquête (1870)*, p. 248.
3. *ADN*, M576/12A.
4. *ADN*, M572/21; E. Lefèvre, *Histoire économique*, pp. 280–1.
5. E. Lefèvre, *L'Industrie lainière*, p. 279.

and absolutely after 1870. Table 7.5 reveals the changing positions of importance of specialist combing and integrated combing concerns.

Table 7.5: Machine combs in Fourmies by type of firm

Year	Specialist combing	Integrated combing
1859[1]	15%	85%
1870[2]	19%	81%
1885[3]	33%	67%
1897[4]	54%	46%

Sources: 1, 3, 4: same as Table 7.4.
          2. *Enquête (1870)*, p. 247.

As in Reims, the shift from integrated to specialist combing entailed a change in the type of technology employed, from the Heilmann machine comb to the Noble or Square Motion machine comb. The use of the latter, however, was virtually confined to one firm, that of Demoulin and Droulers. This specialist combing concern was originally instigated by Holden in the 1870s on an experimental basis, in an attempt to determine the impact on the market of a wider diffusion of his Square Motion machine comb.[41] The firm was successful immediately, and in the first two decades of its existence, it increased its market share at an astonishing rate. In 1885, for example, Demoulin and Droulers was one of a total of six specialist combing concerns in Fourmies, and accounted for 25 per cent of the combing capacity of this type of firms, but only 8 per cent of the combing capacity of the entire worsted industry in the town. By 1897, however, the firm dominated the whole woolcombing sector; it accounted for 95 per cent of the combing capacity of the specialist firms and 51 per cent of the overall total.[42] The success of Demoulin and Droulers in Fourmies and the similar achievement of the Holden enterprise in Reims indicated, above all else, the considerable strength of the commission system of combing.

Commission combing was well established in Bradford when Isaac Holden first began producing combed wool in St. Denis. Although he did not initially follow this practice in France, Holden became committed to it, and after 1851 he combed wool only on commission.[43] The system was straightforward in its operation, though complex in its organisation. Customers delivered their consignment of raw wool to the commission comber, and after the appropriate treatment received back top, noil and waste, paying a commission price on the amount of top produced. The success of the combing operation depended, therefore, on the efficiency with which the machinery combed the raw wool and the guarantee that the customer would be returned his own wool. The sustained expansion of a commission combing enterprise required a relationship of trust between comber and customer.

Writing retrospectively of his experiences in combing, Isaac Holden took credit for perfecting (or even introducing) this system of combing into France. Of the mills in Croix and Reims, he said:

> The construction of these mills is worthy of a passing notice. It was *novel* in the combing world. The whole arrangement and mode of construction for economy of work and the prevention of mixes of the work of different clients were as good as novel and not inferior in these respects to the machinery for washing, carding and combing.[44]

Though some modern authorities have supported Holden's claims, in fact, combing on a commission basis was practised in France, both in the handcombing and embryonic machine combing sector before Holden's arrival.[45] Woolcombing in Tourcoing and in Paris in the 1840s, for example, was organised in this fashion;[46] but there is no doubt that Holden, from the 1850s, developed the commission system to its greatest potential. It should also be emphasised that until the 1870s and the early 1880s, commission combing (on a mechanised basis) was uncommon in most of the major worsted producing areas of France, with the exception of Roubaix, Tourcoing and Holden's factories in Croix and Reims. This was partly for historic reasons as specialist combing on a commission basis had been characteristic practice in Tourcoing before mechanisation, but was virtually unknown elsewhere; and partly because Reims and Fourmies specialised in the production of pure merino worsted goods, for which the Heilmann comb and the integrated spinning and combing organisation were most appropriate.

By 1880, however, the commission system was assuming a greater importance within the worsted industry. In Reims, commission combing grew by default, as the combing operations of many integrated mills were ended during the depression; but in Fourmies, the growth was associated with an overall expansion in the industry. In 1870, a report of the Fourmies Chamber of Commerce remarked that most spinners in the region produced yarn for their own account: but in 1892, independent production was clearly on the decline, as some 60 per cent of the region's worsted spindles spun yarn on commission.[47] At the end of the century, despite the overall predominance of commission combing and the strength of the enterprises of Holden and Demoulin and Droulers, the practice in both Reims and Fourmies was in decline. At the same time, Roubaix and Tourcoing, maintaining their specialisation in commission combing, had become France's main centres of woolcombing.

The data in table 7.6 reveal the rate of growth of Roubaix's woolcombing sector. Until the 1870s, this was similar to that of Fourmies, but less than that of Reims. From the late 1870s to the turn of the century, however, capacity expanded in Roubaix while it contracted in Reims and Fourmies.

Table 7.6: Machine combs in Roubaix, 1853–1903

Year	Number
1853	46
1860	190
1867	356
1878	383
1894	754
1903	1037a

Sources: 1853: B91/5.
1860: Calculated from C. Fohlen, *L'Industrie textile*, p. 232, and *ADN*, M653/28.
1867: *Exposition (1867)*, p. 108.
1878 etc.: *Rapports de la ville* (1879), p. 113; (1895), p. 353; (1904), p. 276, and B-79.

Note: a. This figure does not include the machines in Croix, for which there is no information; all other figures are inclusive of Croix.

In 1901, it was estimated that France produced 61 million kg of combed wool, of which the commission combers of Croix, Roubaix and Tourcoing processed 85 per cent. The two Holden enterprises in Reims and Demoulin and Droulers in Fourmies accounted for most of the remainder.[48] French woolcombing, at the turn of the century, was thus dominated by commission combing, its associated technology – the Noble and the Square Motion machine comb – and by its primary locations, Roubaix and Tourcoing.

It has already been shown that the history of woolcombing mechanisation in nineteenth-century France was influenced by Holden's distinct activities in patent ownership before and after the 1870s. In Roubaix, for instance, the growth in the number of machine combs before the 1870s reflected the diffusion of the Heilmann machine comb. Combers in Roubaix, however, preferred the machine combs controlled by Holden, but before the 1870s were largely unable to meet this preference. Two of the largest concerns, Amédée Prouvost and Camille Leroux, managed to secure several Noble machine combs from the short-lived firm of Tavernier, Crofts and Donisthorpe before Holden purchased the patent and the right to manufacture the machine from them. Unfortunately for Prouvost and Leroux, their purchases were deemed to be included in the provisions of the agreement between Holden and Donisthorpe, and they were thus obliged to pay the stiff licence fee to Holden.[49] The restricted access to woolcombing technology that was reflected in this and other episodes was a constant source of irritation to the combers of Roubaix. On several notable occasions, they attempted to negotiate a way around the licence fees and the patents, but without success.[50] The chance to compete with Holden on equal terms did not occur until the expiry of the most significant patents in the 1870s, when the Square Motion and the Noble machine combs became more widely available.[51]

Although insufficient information exists to explore in detail the diffusion of the Square Motion and the Noble machine combs after 1870, it is clear that both machines became widely used.[52] Until 1867, when there were probably 15 Heilmann machine combs for every Square Motion or Noble machine comb, the Heilmann machine comb was the most widely used woolcombing technology in France. By 1896, after the expiry of the pertinent patents, the Square Motion and Noble machine combs were more extensively used than the Heilmann machine comb. In the Nord *departement*, for example, 60 per cent of the machine combs were of the Square Motion or Noble variety, while the proportion for the country as a whole was 55 per cent.[53]

Other, less quantitative sources also testify to the accelerating diffusion of the Square Motion and Noble machine combs. Norman Holden Crothers, for example, the last manager of the Croix factory, stated that the Square Motion machine comb was adopted by most French combing mills and was erroneously called in France 'Peigneuse Lister'.[54] A senior mechanic with a major machine-making firm in Roubaix reported in 1889 that he was responsible for installing Holden's machine combs in every major worsted producing area in France, as well as in Belgium and Germany.[55] The closure, in 1908, of three combing plants in Roubaix and Fourmies, which disposed of 65 Square Motion and 90 Noble machine combs,[56] further suggests the widespread use of these machines.[57]

Both the technical and organisational features of the woolcombing industry in France changed considerably after 1870. The relaxation of restrictions on the availability of differing woolcombing technologies meant that Holden operated within a quite different competitive context. While his factories were no longer immune from competition, they continued to dominate the industry and remained, throughout the period, the largest concerns of their type in France.

The factories in Croix and Reims were purpose-built (after their potential had been carefully considered) and began with a sizeable concentration of labour and capital. Despite some similarities between the two factories, their performances varied because of differing local conditions and styles of management. The Reims factory, for instance, employed 350 workers within five years of opening – more than twice the number of the closest rival.[58] After extensive growth in the 1850s and 1860s, it became the city's largest industrial employer. In 1863, the firm's assets were officially valued at 1.1. million francs, 50 per cent more than those of the second largest concern in Reims.[59] As the data in Table 7.7 reveal, the firm consolidated this position with additions to the stock of labour and capital before 1890, after which the levels were maintained.

Table 7.7: Isaac Holden Reims factory – labour and capital stock

	Labour	Machine combs
1853[1]	?	12
1858[2]	350	?
1868[3]	?	96
1874[4]	1100	?
1886[5]	1044	107
1890[6]	1062	139

Sources: 1. B–69.
            2. *ADM*, 191M3.
            3. B–13.
            4. *HIL*, p. 498.
            5. G–1.
            6. B–79.

From 1860, the Holden factory in Croix was consistently larger than its counterpart in Reims. It was also more extensive than similar concerns in Roubaix and Tourcoing, as the data in Tables 7.8 and 7.9

Table 7.8: Average size of labour force in woolcombing factories, Croix, Roubaix and Tourcoing, 1855–1900

	Croix	Roubaix	Tourcoing
1855–59	217	92 (6)[a]	31 (6)
1860–64	549	123 (13)	61 (12)
1865–69	834	183 (10)	100 (12)
1870–74	1233	233 (8)	?
1875–79	2000	359 (7)	?
1880–84	1957	316 (9)	122 (10)
1885–89	1693	440 (9)	164 (10)
1890–94	1785	?	?
1895–1900	1690	623 (10)	365 (16)

Sources: ADN, M547/14, 16, 20, 22; M653/24–36, 42, 45; M572/8, 10, 11; M594/1, M619/3, 9: *AN*, F12 4523A (IV): *AMR*, Fv/7: *Rapports de la ville*, (1881), p. 153; (1882), p. 166.
Note: a. Number of concerns given in parentheses.

show. Until the 1870s, the Croix factory expanded at an extremely rapid pace; thereafter the size of the labour force remained constant while the stock of capital grew slowly. The other combing factories in Roubaix and Tourcoing, however, continued to expand well into the twentieth century and their ability to compete with Holden altered substantially during the last quarter of the nineteenth century. Indeed, by 1900, several combing factories in Roubaix, were, in terms of the size of their labour force, similar to Holden's factory in Croix.[60]

Table 7.9: Average number of machine combs in Croix and Roubaix per firm, 1853–90

	Croix	Roubaix
1853	15	8
1868	74	36
1877	121	55
1884	161	?
1888	186	?
1890	190	75

Sources: Croix (in chronological order): B–69; B–13; B–84; G–2; G–1; B–79. Roubaix: as in Table 7.6 (dates approximate) and *Rapports de la ville.*

Within 50 years, therefore, woolcombing in France had been dramatically transformed from a diffused hand process to a massively concentrated modern industry, outpacing other stages of worsted production.[61] While equivalent changes were taking place generally in Europe's industrial structure during this period, the structural and technical changes in French woolcombing were by no means inevitable. There is no doubt that the nature and extent of the progress in French woolcombing was influenced by the inventive and commercial activities of Isaac Holden.

The large scale of woolcombing enterprises was determined by the considerable capital costs of woolcombing both fixed and circulating. Machine combs were the single most expensive item of fixed capital in worsted production. Michel Alcan, professor of textile technology at the Conservatoire Nationale des Arts et Métiers in Paris, published a revealing comparison of production costs in a typical spinning unit and in a typical combing mill in the early 1870s. He estimated that the initial fixed costs of a spinning mill fitted with 6400 worsted spindles capable of producing 100,000 kg of yarn annually were 262,280 francs.[62] At the time of writing, such a mill would have been considered large, being equivalent to an average spinning mill in Roubaix or Fourmies, but perhaps as much as one-third larger than a typical mill in Reims.[63] As for woolcombing, Alcan estimated that the initial fixed costs of a plant using 20 machine combs capable of producing 195,000 kg of combed wool annually were 359,143 francs.[64] In fact, this was unrealistically small as most specialist combing mills, if not the combing plants in integrated mills, typically employed at least two or three times this number of machine combs.[65]

Despite the underestimation in the case of combing, these comparative figures indicate that entry into woolcombing by the 1870s was financially difficult.[66] Although entry was rather easier in the initial stages of the development of French woolcombing, expansion was so rapid that within a decade the size of enterprise was so large as to make the cost of entry prohibitive.[67] In Roubaix, for example, from the 1870s to the turn of the century, the number of woolcombing concerns remained constant, while the industry expanded by increasing its scale of activity.

It has been emphasised throughout this study that Holden's ownership of several significant patents gave him considerable powers. He was able to influence the industry's business rules, particularly with respect to volume and diversity of output, and scale and organisation of production. The rapid diffusion of the Heilmann machine comb during the 1850s and 1860s, for instance, and the concomitant expansion of integrated spinning and combing concerns was partly a defensive response to Holden's power over the market for woolcombing technology. Where specialist combers operated in direct competition to Holden – as in Roubaix – it was necessary that their enterprises be large and reap maximum economies of scale. This placed impediments to entry into the industry and thus concentrated combing capacity into few hands.[68] The characteristic features of combing – those of massive scale and high concentration – remained unchanged after the predominant patents had expired.

Throughout the age of mechanical woolcombing, therefore, the average size of firm was large relative to the overall size of the woolcombing sector. Holden ensured that this situation was maintained by restricting the technology from the outset. There is no doubt that had he permitted the sale of his machine combs directly or through licensing agreements, entry into the industry would have been more common and on a smaller scale. As a result, there would have been a greater variety of firm size.

The organisation of woolcombing production, therefore, was influenced not by the respective technical features of the machine combs, but by the nature of the market of this technology.[69] There was nothing intrinsic in the various technologies that determined their particular organisations. Organisational forms emerged in response to the patent restrictions of the period.[70]

It has been argued that combing became a specialist activity because it was inherently complex and thus required the whole-hearted attention of a single enterprise.[71] It is more likely, however, that woolcombing became complex because it was specialised, rather than the reverse. The relatively small combing plants integrated with spinning mills that existed in Reims and Fourmies in the 1850s and 1860s support this view. This form of organisation operated satisfactorily in the absence of competition from the specialist comber or during periods of rapid expansion in the industry, and declined only when the market for woolcombing technology changed.

Isaac Holden came to France at an opportune moment in the development of the French worsted industry. Inspired by his partner, Samuel Cunliffe Lister, during the first decade of his business career in France, Holden maintained his dominance in woolcombing by combining technical leadership (through the Square Motion and patent interference in other machine combs) and great organisational and management skills. Through these qualities, Holden was able to turn out a superior product. His factories in Reims and Croix were the marvel of the period, and although they were unique for some time, their structure was finally copied as the standard for the entire woolcombing industry. Though Holden stated modestly on more than one occasion that he desired simply a solid family business, he achieved much more than this. In fulfilling his aim to provide a stable income for his heirs, Holden exerted a powerful and enduring influence on the French woolcombing industry.

Notes

1   Holden's testimony appears in *Enquête industrielle sur le traité de commerce avec l'Angleterre* (Paris, 1860), vol. 3, p. 480. Between 1860 and 1876, France granted 29 patents for woolcombing machinery while England granted 136 patents.
2   A. Falleur, *L'Industrie lainière dans la région de Fourmies* (Paris, 1930), p. 26.
3   *Exposition universelle de 1851: Travaux de la commission française* (Paris, 1854), vol. IV, p. 214: C. Fohlen, *L'Industrie textile au temps du second empire* (Paris, 1956), p. 113.
4   W. O. Henderson, *Britain and Industrial Europe 1750–1870* (Leicester, 1965), p. 84.
5   *Exposition (1851)*, pp. 142–3.
6   M. Chevalier (ed.), *Exposition universelle de 1867 à Paris: Rapports du Jury International* (Paris, 1868), vol. IV, p. 108.
7   *Statistique de la France* (Paris, 1847), vol. I, pp. 174–5. The only exception to this was the firm Pradine and Company which in the 1840s was reported as a combing concern; the firm experimented with early machine combs. See *Statistique (1847)* p. 175 and *Exposition (1851)*, p. 142. In the 1850s they were reported as spinners and combers. *ADM*, 191M4.
8   The mechanisation of combing in Reims had far-reaching effects on handcombing in the countryside around Reims. In and around Châlons-

sur-Marne and especially in the Suippes valley handcombing struggled on during the 1850s; but it had apparently disappeared in both localities by 1860. *ADM*, 186M7.

9   A report from the Chamber of Commerce of Reims in July 1858 remarked on the changes which had occurred in the organisation of production of the local worsted industry: 'not long ago, almost all the spinners worked on commission, the combed wool being supplied to them by merchants. Mechanical combing has changed this state of affairs. A number of spinners have added mechanical combing to their spinning mills and now produce yarn for their own account which they sell to the "fabrique".' See *ADM*, 172M3. D. M. Gordon, 'Merchants and Capitalists: Industrialization and Provincial Politics at Reims and St Etienne under the Second Republic and Second Empire' (Ph.D. Brown University, Providence, 1978), p. 117; J. Turgan, *Les Grandes usines: études industrielles en France et à l'etranger* (Paris, 1868), vol. 8, p. 70.

10 During most of the second half of the nineteenth century, there were only two specialist combing concerns in Reims. *ADM*, 191M4.

11 Falleur, *L'industrie lainière*, p. 26.

12 *Ibid.*, p. 27.

13 *Enquête parlementaire sur le régime économique* (Paris, 1870), p. 246.

14 *ADN*, M653/27.

15 *Ibid.*

16 *Enquête (1870)*, p. 246.

17 *ADN*, M653/34.

18 According to official records, the number of handcombers reached a peak in 1856 with a total of 2785 workers organised by 66 merchant/master combers; at the same time, there were four machine combing concerns employing 127 workers. *ADN*, M653/24. Ten years later, the number of handcombers had fallen to 243 with nine merchant/master combers while the number of machine combing concerns had risen to 12 employing 1258 workers. *ADN*, M653/33.

19 Fohlen, *L'industrie textile*, p. 227 and A. Goblet, *Le Peignage de la laine à Roubaix-Tourcoing et son évolution économique et sociale* (Lille, 1903), p. 68.

20 B91/5.

21 *Ibid.*, and *Patents for Inventions Granted in France from 1791 to 1876 Inclusive: Subject Matter Index* (Washington, 1883), p. 198.

22 B-91/5.

23 *Ibid.*

24 This is calculated on the basis of data given in G. Duveau, *La Vie ouvrière en France sous le second empire* (Paris, 1946), p. 168; *ADN*, M547/5; B-91/5.

25 See Chapter 2, pp. 15–16. The Hubner machine comb patented on 27 August 1851 had similar beginnings and was manufactured by another of Alsace's leading industrialists, André Koechlin, *Histoire documentaire de l'industrie de Mulhouse et de ses environs au XIXe siècle* (Mulhouse, 1902), p. 230.

26 A typical case is Legrand of Fourmies whose firm was totally integrated employing 14 Heilmann machine combs, 10,200 worsted spindles and 125 power looms (there were an additional 800–1500 handlooms) in 1870. Worsted spinners who testified at the Parliamentary enquiry in 1870 confirmed their use of Heilmann's machine comb (the evidence of Hartmann, Reichard and Company of Erstein – Bas-Rhin, and Tranchard and Company of Neuville reporting on the worsted industry in Rethel). See *Enquête (1870)*, pp. 151, 154, 167.

27 M. Alcan, *Fabrication des étoffes: Traité du travail des laines peignées* (Paris, 1873), pp. 249, 267. These ratios are confirmed by the records of Holden's

factories; *Enquête (1870)*, p. 248; *Enquête (1860)* p. 487; and H. Priestman, *Principles of Wool Combing* (London, 1921) p. 193.

28   This statement is based on a detailed breakdown of the spindlage of worsted spinning mills in Reims in 1860 giving an average of 3600 spindles per mill. *ADM*, 187M17; and Alcan, *Fabrication des étoffes*, p. 456.

29   *Enquête (1860)*, pp. 484, 486. This strategy eroded the fears expressed by both Angus and Jonathan Holden. The former dreaded the day when Heilmann's patent expired because he saw it as an open invitation to the resurgence of many systems of combing which had remained dormant during the life of the patent. *HIL*, pp. 261–2. Jonathan, Isaac Holden's nephew and manager of the Reims factory, was more concerned about balancing the cost of buying the patent from Nicolas Schlumberger with the likely revenues from being its licensee. Jonathan Holden to Isaac Crothers, 26 June 1861 (L–VIII/2).

30   *Enquête (1860)*, vol. 3, pp. 485–7; B–65 being Isaac Holden's notes to the Chevalier Commission on the Anglo-French Treaty; Jonathan Holden to Isaac Crothers, 19 January 1861 (L–VIII/2).

31   *Enquête (1860)*, vol. 3, p. 486.

32   One commission comber who employed the Noble machine exclusively was Thuillier-Gelée of Amiens, a long-standing customer of Holden's. The firm began in 1857 using Noble machines half of which were made in France and half in England. See *Enquête (1870)*, p. 150. The conclusion about the impact of the licence fee is based on Alcan, *Fabrication des étoffes*, p. 248 and profit figures from Holden's factories given in Appendix, Table A.1, and from Amédée Prouvost and Company, given in Fohlen, *L'Industrie textile*, pp. 337, 400.

33   During these years, Holden received 5000 francs as a licence fee for every Heilmann machine constructed and sold by Nicolas Schlumberger. *Enquête (1860)*, vol. 3, p. 487. The agreement signed with Schlumberger did not restrict the availability of the machine (B–91/8 and L–I).

34   Jonathan Holden to Isaac Crothers, 14 April 1860 (L–VIII/1).

35   See Appendix, Figure A3.

36   Jonathan Holden to Isaac Crothers, 19 November 1867 (B–5B); Angus Holden to Isaac Holden, 30 June 1869 (B–13); Fohlen, *L'Industrie textile*, pp. 344, 443.

37   See Appendix A–3.

38   See Appendix A–1.

39   E. Lefevre, *L'industrie lainière actuelle* (Reims, 1912), p. 235.

40   *Ibid.*, p. 239.

41   Jonathan Holden to Isaac Holden, 23 October 1875 (B–15A).

42   The firm employed 42 Square Motion machine combs in 1885. *ADN*, M576/12A and M572/21. Lefèvre argues that Holden's 'machinisme' accounts for the general demise of woolcombing in Fourmies during this period. Lefèvre, *L'industrie lainière*, p. 278.

43   Turgan, *Les Grandes usines*, p. 103 (B–60).

44   B–77, p. 9.

45   Henderson, *Britain and Industrial Europe*, p. 101; D. T. Jenkins and K.G. Ponting, *The British Wool Textile Industry 1770–1914* (London, 1982), p. 336.

46   For Tourcoing see A. Chanut *et al.* 'Le département du Nord', in E. Labrousse (ed.), *Aspects de la crise et de la dépression de l'économie française au milieu du XIXe siècle, 1846–1851* (La Roche-sur-Yon, 1956), p. 110. In Paris, on the eve of the 1848 Revolution, 14 of 22 specialist combing concerns worked exclusively on commission. *Statistique de l'industrie à Paris* (Paris, 1851), pp. 415–18.

47   *Enquête (1870)*, p. 247, and *ADN*, M571/47.

48 J. H. Clapham, *The Woollen and Worsted Industries* (London, 1907), p. 224. Reporting to the Tariff Commission in 1899, Gaston Grandgeorge remarked that: 'all of the wool going to the worsted mills pass by the 6 or 8 large combing concerns in Croix, Roubaix, Tourcoing, Reims and in the region of Fourmies.' G. Grandgeorge, *Ministère du commerce et de l'industrie. Commission permanente des valeurs de douane; les industries textiles de la France en 1898* (Paris, 1899), p. 60.

49 L-I.

50 In August 1861, Amédée Prouvost devised an elaborate scheme to crush the rival firm of Morel, an act which would benefit all the combers in Roubaix including Holden in Croix. The price to Holden for this was to drop the licence fee for six Noble machine combs. The plan was never put into action. Isaac Crothers to Isaac Holden, 5 August 1861 (L-VIII/2).

51 The Square Motion machine comb was not immune from attempts to pirate its technology. At the end of 1869, Jonathan Holden learned that a prominent Roubaisien machine-maker had constructed a number of imitation Square Motion machine combs infringing the current patents. Amédée Prouvost managed to secure 16 of these, Allart-Rousseau had 4 and Vinchon and Morel 3 each. The outcome of this incident is unknown but it must be assumed that the machines were dismantled. See Jonathan Holden to Isaac Holden, 18 November 1869 (B-7B); Isaac Crothers to Isaac Holden, 2 December 1869 (*HIL*, p. 434). On another occasion in 1876, Jonathan Holden ended what he suspected to be an attempt by Delattre, a leading worsted spinner to corner the market on constructing the Square Motion once the relevant patents had expired. See Jonathan Holden to Isaac Holden, 22 September 1876 (B-71). For a long time, Holden had his Square Motion machine comb constructed and experimented with in England or, in some cases, assembled in France from parts made in both France and England (B-77, p. 10). While in St Denis, Holden imported an assortment of machinery from England including spinning equipment (*AN*, F12 4803-11). Isaac Crothers constantly expressed his optimism concerning the working of the Square Motion and, by definition, the lack of such an outlook by the rival combers of Roubaix. See, for example, Isaac Crothers to Isaac Holden, 14 July 1865 and 29 December 1865 (both in L-VIII/6).

52 Despite claims to the contrary. See, for example, Clapham, *Woollen and Worsted Industries*, p. 41.

53 *Annuaire Statistique*, vol. 17 (1897), p. 155.

54 Notes by N. H. Crothers, October 1958 (G-3).

55 *AMR*, FII (b)/7.

56 *United Kingdom: Foreign Office, Consular Reports*, n. 4264 (1908).

57 A visit to the combing plant of A. Motte (Roubaix) revealed 150 Heilmann type, 72 Lister and 42 Noble combs. See W. A. Graham Clark, *Manufacture of Woolen, Worsted and Shoddy in France and England and Jute in Scotland* (Washington, 1909), House of Representatives Document 1330, p. 21.

58 *ADM*, 191M3.

59 *ADM*, 186M8 and 191M14.

60 In 1867, the labour force in six combing factories in Roubaix ranged between 20 and 300 - the latter represented the firm of Morel. Prouvost employed 293 workers at this time (*ADN*, M655/11). In 1880 Holden employed 2250 workers; the corresponding figure for Morel was 1400; for Prouvost, 1200; and for Vinchon, 1200 (*ADN*, M619/3). In 1904, the four largest combers in Roubaix each employed more than 1000 workers (*ADN*, M607/38).

61 According to the census of 1896, 50 per cent of the worsted spinning mills

in the Nord employed more than 100 workers; the corresponding figure in combing was 85 per cent. One-third of the combing factories in the *département* employed more than 500 workers. See *Ministère du Commerce, de l'industrie, des postes et des telegraphes. Résultats statistiques du recensement des industries et professions. Dénombrement Général de la population du 29 mars 1896* (Paris, 1901), p. 553. In Roubaix in 1904, the average size of the labour force in the city's combing, spinning and weaving (worsted) mills was 482, 200 and 227, respectively (*ADN*, M607/38). In the 1898 Tariff Commission Report, Gaston Grandgeorge remarked upon the significant changes which had taken place in woolcombing since it was mechanised: 'woolcombing was once attached to the spinning mill ... today it is no longer the same, woolcombing plants working no longer for spinners, or at least only in exceptional cases, but for those who trade in wool, selling their wool no longer in the raw state but as top' (Grandgeorge, *Les Industries textiles*, p. 60). Letters exchanged between Isaac Holden and Isaac Crothers after 1870 confirm the increasing importance of the topmaker. This change had the effect of involving combers in the international wool market and introducing speculative interest – a futures market in combed wool, for example, was opened in Roubaix in 1888. G. Franchomme, 'L'évolution démographique et économique de Roubaix dans le dernier tiers du XIXe siècle', *Revue du Nord*, 51 (1969), p. 30; G. Graham Clark, House of Representatives Document 1330, p. 11; *United Kingdom: Foreign Office*, Consular Reports, n. 2582 (1900), pp. 23–4; M. Mussault, *Histoire du marché à terme en laines peignées de Roubaix–Tourcoing* (Paris, 1909). As a distinct industrial activity within worsted production, woolcombing enjoyed a considerable export trade during the second half of the nineteenth century. Combined exports of combed and carded wool (as a per cent of total output) increased dramatically from 1.6 per cent in 1850 to 32.5 per cent before World War I. Combing and carding also earned considerably more foreign exchange than did both the spinning and weaving sectors; in the last quarter of the century, for example, export earnings of combed and carded wool doubled while those of yarn and cloth fell substantially. For the relevant data, see T. J. Markovitch, 'L'industrie française de 1789 à 1964', *Cahiers de L'ISEA*, ser. AF, 6 (1966), Table XVI.

62   Alcan, *Fabrication des étoffes*, pp, 451–2.

63   *Enquête (1870)*, p. 159.

64   Alcan, *Fabrication des étoffes*, p. 270.

65   See this Chapter, p. 90.

66   *ADN*, M653/27; the same applied in Tourcoing (*ADN*, M653/28).

67   In Roubaix, in 1859, enterprises opening during the year were consistently larger than those already established. Between the first and third quarter of the year, the number of woolcombing firms increased from 9 to 13, while the labour each employed increased from 80 to 112. See *ibid*.

68   A. Picard, *Le Bilan d'un siècle, 1801–1900* (Paris, 1906) vol. 4, p. 352.

69   The following section draws on ideas presented by W. Lazonick, 'Industrial Organization and Technological Change: the Decline of the British Cotton Industry', *Business History Review*, 57 (1983), pp. 195–236.

70   The American worsted industry was highly integrated yet employed the Noble machine comb. See P. T. Cherington, *The Wool Industry* (New York, 1916), p. 7.

71   Clapham, *Woollen and Worsted*, p. 137; Jenkins and Ponting, *The British Wool Industry*, p. 178.

72   *Ibid*.

8 Conclusion

The mechanisation of combing was the last major textile innovation of the Industrial Revolution. The solution to the problem of machine combing was technically consistent with the mechanisation of spinning and weaving which had preceded it. All of these innovations basically consisted of the imitation and substituion of hand processes by machinery. As in spinning and (to a lesser extent) weaving, the mechanisation of combing had considerable impact on the structure of employment destroying a traditionally organised handicraft industry on the one hand, and adding to a growing population of factory-disciplined workers on the other. Yet, because of the lateness of the innovation, roughly 70 years after the breakthrough in machine spinning, and 20 or 30 years after a similar move in machine weaving, the mechanisation of combing differed fundamentally from the other textile innovations and, consequently, its impact on worsted production generally was unlike that of earlier innovations.

When Heilmann, Holden, Lister and Noble made their distinct (and nearly simultaneous) contributions to machine combing, they were able to draw on a considerable body of technical knowledge primarily in mechanical engineering and machine-tool technology to bring their ideas to fruition. Thus they were able to design and construct their respective machines with a degree of tolerance denied to their forebears. It is primarily for this reason that the machine combs of the 1850s had such a high degree of perfection which was not substantially altered over the following half-century. At the same time, important advances in transport, especially in railways, made it possible to move the considerable and concentrated amount of output which these machines were capable of producing under factory conditions. Finally, and not least significant, thanks to the solid establishment of labour discipline and factory organisation, machine combs were able to be put to work quickly and achieve immediate results.

The context allowing for successful mechanisation was thus already in place before machine woolcombing began and, therefore, the revolutionary effects which, for example, characterised the mechanisation of spinning, were largely absent here.

But it was primarily in the degree and mechanism of its diffusion that woolcombing technology differed from previous innovations in textile production. No earlier textile innovation was so intimately bound to the patent system, nor especially to the burgeoning international patent system. Moreover, the patent had never been so effectively exploited as a tool of industrial capitalism to create such acute concentrations, or even monopolies of technology. The complicated negotiations between Lister, Holden, Donisthorpe and Schlumberger during the middle of the nineteenth century, which were examined in detail in an earlier chapter, were not simply an aspect of industrial competition. Rather, the exchange of patent rights at the heart of the negotiations sealed the technical history of woolcombing for at least half a century, for better or for worse; and, as we have seen, it also dictated the precise nature of the organisation of woolcombing production. The wide range of technological approaches and organisational forms which had prevailed in woolcombing were thus drastically reduced. Subsequent technical changes in woolcombing were judiciously controlled; their degree of success depended as much on the measures employed, both legal and organisational, to protect the existing technologies as upon any need to improve them.

The mechanisation of woolcombing is best understood as part of the process of the growth of large-scale enterprise, concentration of production and intense competition and protection of industrial innovations characteristic of European industrial capitalism in the latter nineteenth century. To find parallel developments in the history of technology, one needs to look at the new science-based industries of the period, when the accumulation and exchange of patent rights and protection became a standard feature of the diffusion of technology and the growth of industrial monopolies.

9   Epilogue

In a study based on the business objectives and activities of two key figures in the history of the mechanisation of woolcombing in France during the second half of the nineteenth century, it is fitting to end with a note on their personal fate. After their relatively short but highly significant partnership, Lister and Holden pursued separate interests, but their paths were to cross again in an acrimonious episode which revealed the unsavoury face of the inventive process.

After his experience in St Denis, Lister focused his attention on his Bradford concern, implicitly ending his interests in Europe and in woolcombing. Manningham Mills, the centre of his operations, continued to prosper as Lister associated himself with a succession of partners. Likewise, his consuming passion for mechanical inventions endured until the end of his life: allegedly he took out over 150 patents for various machines not all of which were for textile processes. Apart from his contributions to the mechanisation of woolcombing, Lister's most lasting invention was a machine for converting silk waste into useable silk products. His business reflected these changing technical interests; the product line was diversified from worsteds and included the manufacture of velvet and carpets. These latter activities brought Lister considerable commercial success and he invested part of his enormous wealth in acquiring land in North Yorkshire, including a large estate at Masham and an estate comprising Jervaulx Abbey. He died in 1906 at the age of 91 having been made first Baron Masham in 1891.

Isaac Holden's life and career progressed differently after the dissolution of the partnership. Though an independent producer and, by then, a wealthy man, Holden did not remain long in France to control directly the daily affairs of his factories. 1860 marked an important turning-point. In the previous year, the factory in St Denis made a substantial loss and, following an enquiry into the causes, it was agreed to end operations there and concentrate production entirely at Croix and Reims. At about the same time, Holden helped establish his sons, Angus and Edward, in business with the purchase of Penny Oak Mills, in Bradford. On a personal level, in the same year, Holden formed an important alliance with the Illingworths, a prominent Bradford family, by a double marriage — his son Angus married Margaret Illingworth, and his daughter Mary married Henry Illingworth.

Holden's attention was thus being drawn back to Bradford from where twelve years earlier he had left in despair. Sarah, his wife, added further pressure for him to leave France — she did not enjoy living in France and, during the family's stay in St Denis, she spent as little time as possible there. Whatever his own inclination was, Holden succumbed to the various influences and, in 1861, after winding up his affairs in St Denis and ensuring himself that the other factories were well settled under the management of his nephews, he returned to Yorkshire.

Ironically, within a very short time of his return to England, Holden fell ill, but recovered quickly. Three years later, in 1864, he opened his main woolcombing concern in Bradford, the Alston Works, but once again he fell ill with an indeterminate complaint. This time he was ordered to rest entirely from business. In the following year, Holden began to cultivate a new pursuit — he was invited to stand as a Liberal candidate for Knaresborough in the forthcoming parliamentary general election. Despite a provocative campaign by the Tory opposition, who seized upon Holden's business success in France and questioned his loyalty to the country, Holden was returned as an MP for the constituency. He held the seat until 1868 when he gave it up to his son-in-law, Alfred Illingworth (who had married Margaret Holden in 1866), in order to contest the East Division of the West Riding. Only Alfred was successful.

For the time being, Holden retired from an active political career: on two occasions, 1872 and 1874, he tried to return to Parliament but was unsuccessful. In 1882, however, he had better luck and became the MP for the North-West Division of the West Riding; and in 1885, he became the MP for the newly-created constituency of Keighley, which he held until 1896.

Both inside and outside of Parliament, Holden supported the Liberal cause and played an important part in the formation of policies, especially those relating to economic matters. At the same time, he gave unswerving support to the Methodist movement, to which he had been loyally committed for a long time. Earlier in his life, he had seriously considered a career as a Methodist clergyman. In France, he was an important and active supporter of the French Wesleyan cause; and at his factories in St Denis, Croix and Reims, he provided his workers with Chapels, Bible classes and other means of satisfying their religious aspirations. In England, Holden offered financial as well as moral support - in 1871, for example, he donated £5000 for the erection of 50 chapels in the London area. Holden also advocated a programme of technical education for the layman and for some time he was President of the Keighley Technical Institute. In recognition of his contributions to the political life of the nation, Holden was granted a baronetcy in 1893.

Holden's pursuit of political, religious and educational interests did not, however, detract from his business commitments. Despite all, he essentially remained a businessman until the end of his life. His nephews and sons may have run the affairs of his extensive business empire, but he gave it inspiration and was, ultimately, its head. No major business decision, in France or in England, was taken without him. But of all the aspects of business that concerned him, nothing fascinated him more than the technology of woolcombing. The Square Motion comb was his pride; he continually sought to improve its performance and was still taking patents out on it in the 1880s. In a letter to his wife in 1861, Isaac Holden expressed a longing for this technology which continued to dominate his mind until his death in 1897:

> I do not seem quite like a man retired. It seems that when I come within the sound of our dear old combing machines, the old passion comes over me and I cannot keep aloof from them.

As for the fate of Holden's business, the Reims factory was destroyed during the First World War and not rebuilt: the Croix factory ceased production in 1938 and its assets sold to the local Syndicat des Peigneurs. The Alston Works continued to operate until 1965 when it was finally incorporated within a large textile combine.

The acrimony between Lister and Holden which infected their association from the outset persisted until the death of both men. The dispute centred on which of the two was the true inventor of the Square Motion machine comb. Lister claimed authorship: Holden maintained he had discovered its substance even before meeting Lister. Initially kept private, the dispute eventually became public when an angry exchange of letters appeared in the local press and was subsequently printed under separate cover as *The Square Motion Combing Machine: Its Origin*. The argument was further exacerbated as a result of the publication of James Burnley's *The History of Wool and Woolcombing* (1889). Burnley's conclusions were not unbiased and made much of Holden's inventive genius. This enraged Lister who subsequently demanded and received a retraction from the author. Lister also retaliated by publishing his own work *Lord Masham's Inventions* (1905), in which he described his own version of the invention of the Square Motion machine comb. It is unlikely that the true identity of its authorship will be ascertained with certainty though modern authorities tend to support Holden's claims. On 13 January 1887, *The Yorkshireman* printed its own version of the disagreements which, because of its poignancy, is reproduced below.

THE ACT-ON-THE-SQUARE MOTION.
A TALE OF AFFRONT AND TWO SIDES.

CHAPTER I.—THE AFFRONT.

Years ago there lived in Worstedopolis two men in the prime and vigour of life who were drawn together by a mutual sympathy for the woolcombing machine, which at that time was far from being a perfect contrivance. The name of one was Sam, the name of the other Ike. The former had been experimenting for some years with the machine in question, and was making money by it; the latter had been *thinking* about the machine for some years, and was *longing* to make money by it. "I can help you," said Ike to Sam. "Let us comb together, then," said Sam. So they combed and came together, and both embarked in the ship called Partnership, Sam being the heavy weight at the helm and Ike the light-weight at the prow. They steered for France, and there the standard of the Woolcomb was planted, and Ike was left behind to guard it while Sam returned to Worstedopolis to look after his other affairs, which his other partners were mixing for him pretty considerably.

A few years elapsed, during which there had sprung into existence a machine to which the name of the Square Motion was given. These few years were years of mystery. Ike was all for the Square Motion, Sam was all for another machine called the Nip. Each got his way, Ike kept the Square Motion going in France while Sam kept the Nip going in England, and so matters went on until Sam's "other affairs" became rather unmanageable, and he was glad to sell out of the French partnership altogether.

Thus Ike became master of the French position and the Square Motion and in course of time made vast wealth, and, as luck and pluck would have it, Sam overcame his difficulties, plunged into fresh ventures, and he too became rich and great.

According to the opinion of the world both had got what they set out to get, and more, and ease and contentment ought to have been theirs for the rest of their lives. But, alas for the perversity of human nature! it was not so.

Both were greatly honoured in the land; Sam had a marble statue erected to him in the park which had once been attached to his ancestral mansion, and Ike was made a member of Parliament. Still they were not happy; at least Sam wasn't, for, having no longer to fight for fortune, he bethought him he would fight for the honour of having invented the Square Motion. And he fought, and he is fighting still, and it is with this Act-on-the-Square fight that this story has to do.

"*I* invented the Square Motion," cried Sam.

"I beg your pardon, it was *my* idea," said Ike.

"But *I* obtained a patent for it," continued Sam.

"To which my name ought to have been attached," added Ike.

"Oh, fiddle o' that tale!"

"Yes, that's just the tale I do mean to fiddle on. And even if you did invent it (which you didn't) you could do nothing with the machine. Did you not abandon it and throw it into the scrap heap?"

"I preferred the Nip, that is all."

"Then why do you make so much fuss about the square motion?"

"Because it has made you wealthy."

"That's the truth. Go to your purpose."

"So I will, and I'll write you down in the papers."

"And write yourself down at the same time."

"What do you mean?"

"Ask Dogberry."

And this constituted the affront.

CHAPTER II.—ONE SIDE. SAM WRITES.

TO THE EDITORS OF THE YORKSHIRE PRESS.

GENTLEMEN,—I am the biggest inventor the world ever saw. I invented everything, that statement included. There is a man called Ike who says he invented the Square Motion. He has had his bust in the Royal Academy; he deserves to have "bust" altogether. My statue in Lister Park laughs at him as he passes by, and he is mad, but I'm going to make him madder. Why, Ike never invented so much as a single screw, though I acknowledge he's drawn my screw considerably by making his pile out of the Square Motion – that is, *my* Square Motion. But I've a better pile than his in my velvet. Let him put that into his pipe and smoke it. *He* invent the Square Motion, indeed! His was the *round* motion, and he got round me with it to a fine tune I can tell you. Honest Jonathan was the man that worked the machine; and I was the master that didn't care a fig for it, being so much Nipped in England. I am a gentlemen, and was born one. I had ancestors. That's one for him. I've lost three fortunes. I've made ten times three fortunes, but this is not enough; no, I had rather lose them all [another invention] than lose the credit of having invented the machine which has made Ike his fortune. Come to my help, Honest Jonathan, and let us smash the proud imposter together. Then this matchless man says he invented the lucifer match. How wonderful! Who patented that, I wonder! But, here, to cut the matter short and conclude this business once and for all, I am willing to stake my Presidency of the Fair Trade League against his M.P.-ship, with £10,000,000 into the bargain, that he cannot prove what is unprovable. If he fails to take up this challenge, then I say what I say is true, and what he says anybody may believe that likes. But it is my proud boast that the whole world knows and believes in Sam, and that Sam's little finger is of more importance than Ike's whole body. That's the way to say it, I laugh, ha! ha! I laugh, ho! ho! I would be dignified if it suited my mood, but it doesn't, so please let me tickle him up. Send me 10,000 slips to distribute amongst my friends. — Yours, &c.,

SAM.

CHAPTER III. — THE OTHER SIDE. IKE WRITES.

DEAR MR. EDITORS. — If Sam will refer to Leviticus xiv., verse -, no, no, I mean to my former letters, dated 1st April, 1815, and 1st April, 1829, respectively, he will find that I have effectually answered everything that he has, can, will, or may bring against me, and that as to his preposterous challenge, I am scarcely the fool (though still but a young man) to accept it when he declined my equally preposterous challenge I don't know how many years ago. I regret I cannot make myself into a story-teller for his benefit, and that he will be so stupid as to reap up these things time after time, when I thrashed him so thoroughly in my former letters. Nothing can shake *them*. Does he forget the famous interview in Hattersley's shop? If he does, let me refer him to - -, but no, I'll have the whole correspondence reprinted, and then the public can refer to it as well. — Yours, &c.,

IKE.

SUPPLEMENT.

(Being an Extract from Public Opinion.)

Who cares? What does it matter? They are both two Grand Old Men. Why doesn't some one make them shake hands? That would be a Square Motion that everybody would like to see invented and patented.

Appendix

Production and Financial Data, Croix and Reims 1853–94

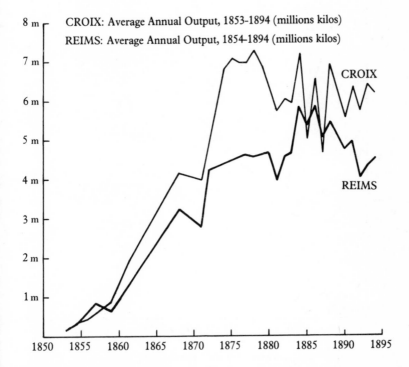

Figure A.1: Output of combed wool at Croix and Reims factories, 1853-94

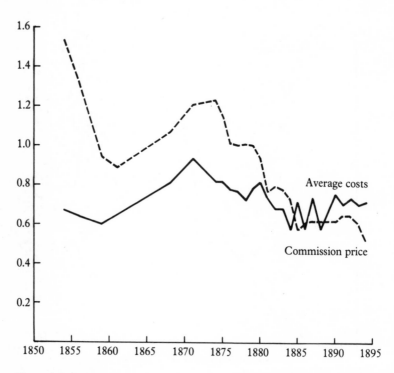

Figure A.2: Commission price and unit costs at Croix factory,
1854-94 (francs/kilo of top)

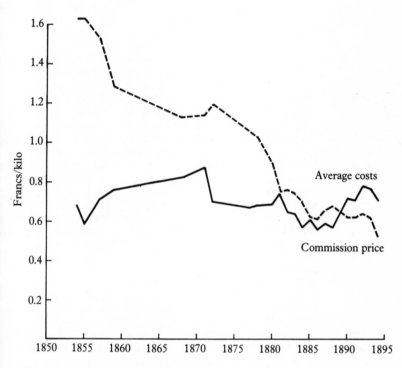

Figure A.3: Commission price and unit costs at Reims factory, 1854–94
(francs/kilo of top)

Table A.1: Trading profit and capital at Croix and Reims factories, 1860–94

	Croix and Reims Trading profits[1] (francs)	Capital[2] (francs)
1860	1,060,135.69	3,892,289.93
1861	791,910.80	4.503,659.62
1862	793,326.19	5.081,068.97

	Croix		Reims	
	Trading profit[1]	Capital[2]	Trading profit[1]	Capital[2]
1863	541,115.43	2,365.434.80	943,639,96	2,461,983.20
1864	645,978.90	2,393,151.26	1,109,051.14	2,339,874.50
1865	539,667.26	2,347,867.37	1,141,971.75	2,351,203.90
1866	681,061.01	2,827,501.78	1,038,577.53	2,679,669.61
1867	525,221.03	3,438,691.94	758,577.10	2,825,079.80
1868	1,291,270.84	3,789,795.92	1,178,029.91	3,500,918.63
1869	1,514,635.31	4,450,943.73	1,300,200.75	3,742,975.44
1870	1,188,455.75	4,764,710.32	881,318.16	3,767,234.20
1871	1,603,569.21	5,507,876.87	1,351,090.63	4,191,080.61
1872	2,341,704.35	5,942,206.23	2,291,196.88	4,118,635.64
1873	2,855,467.54	8,033,705.73	2,004,080.41	4,277,570.27
1874	3,326,397.53	9,925,048.67	2,157,856.09	4,258,897.38
1875	2,586,818.15	10,159,804.88	1,654,696.27	4,493,045.82
1876	2,887,842.36	10,307,758.75	1,695,409.77	4,708,142.29
1877	2,864,974.16	9,538,226.10	1,969,511.09	4,738,770.05
1878	2,962,589.73	9,712,488.51	—	5,047,469.84
1879	2,833,263.47	10,971,073.19	—	—
1880	1,875,520.89	11,292,675.76	2,149,957.61	—
1881	1,245,629.39	12,715,826.10	471,011.32	6,001,165.51
1882	1,965,958.22	13,509,412.24	1,003,568.57	6,476,672.23
1883	1,938,416.50	14,430,956.16	1,093,228.30	7,464,565.60
1884	1,634,958.47	14,480,258.75	1,383,646.45	8,628,921.82
1885	393,545.67	15,712,929.74	763,437.10	9,627,632.82
1886	1,071,775.76	15,575,782.61	1,142,043.30	10,017,774.27
1887	303,558.51	15,728,572.57	941,895.37	10,210,318.67
1888	1,261,970.40	15,631,702.58	1,069,501.59	10,489,933.34
1889	—	16,378,648.30	—	10,712,768.63
1890	1,091,452.36	14,416,521.57	305,324.64	9,675,943.52
1891	849,577.35	14,803,234.60	304,540.18	9,831,140.41
1892	530,337.83	14,457,070.35	−34,613.43	9,868,786.04
1893	536,547.08	14,242,541.00	−59,846.00	9,308,201.16
1894	−182,531.57	14,510,814.53	−302,429.79	9,540,906.16

Notes: 1. Before interest on capital was deducted, as of 31 December.
2. As of 31 December of the previous year.

Sources: As in Table 5.1.

Bibliography

Archives

Archives Nationales, Paris
Series F12
Archives Départementales de la Marne, Châlons-sur-Marne
Series M
Archives Départementales du Nord, Lille
Series M
Archives Départementales de la Seine, Paris
Series $D^{10}U^3$, $D^{31}U^3$
Archives Municipales de Croix
Series F
Archives Municipales de Roubaix
Series F
Rapports sur l'administration et la situation des affaires de la ville
de Roubaix pendant l'année (1873–1910)
Archives Municipales de St Denis
Series F
University of Bradford, Bradford
Holden Papers
University of Leeds, Leeds
Holden Business Archive
Privately Held Papers, London and East Grinstead, Sussex

Printed Material

Alcan, M., *Essai sur l'industrie des matières textiles,* (Paris, 1847)

Alcan, M., *Fabrications des étoffes. Traité du travail des laines peignées, de l'alpaga, du poil, de la chèvre, du cachemire, etc.,* (Paris, 1873)

Annuaire Statistique

Annuaire Statistique du Département du Nord

Ballot, C., *L'Introduction du machinisme dans l'industrie française,* (Paris, 1923)

Barnard, A., *The Australian Wool Market 1840-1900,* (Melbourne, 1958)

Bergeron, L., *Les Capitalistes en France 1780-1914,* (Paris, 1978).

Bergeron, L., 'Douglas, Ternaux, Cockerill: aux origines de la mécanisation de l'industrie lainière en France', *Revue Historique* 247 (1970), 67-80

Bird, D. J., 'The Holden Comb', B. Tech. dissertation, University of Bradford (1971)

Bulletin de la Société d'encouragement pour l'industrie nationale, (Paris, 1802-)

Bulletin de la Société industrielle de Mulhouse, (Mulhouse, 1826-)

Burnley, J., *The History of Wool and Woolcombing,* (London, 1889)

Byles, F., and A. J. Best, *The Holden-Illingworth Letters,* (Bradford, 1927)

Cadet, F., *Société industrielle de Reims: Conférence de 1867-1868,* (Reims, 1869)

Cameron, R. E., *France and the Economic Development of Europe 1800-1914,* (Princeton, 1961)

Cameron, R. E. and C. E. Freedman, 'French Economic Growth: A Radical Revision', *Social Science History* 7 (1983), 3-30

Chambre de Commerce de Reims, *Exposition Universelle à Vienne, 1873: Notes sur Reims et le département de la Marne,* (Reims, 1873)

Chevalier, M. (ed.), *Exposition Universelle de 1867: Rapports du Jury International,* (Paris, 1868)

A. Chanut et al., 'Aspects industriels de la crise: le département du Nord', in E. Labrousse, *Aspects de la crise et de la dépression de l'économie française au milieu du XIXe siècle 1846-51,* (La Roche-sur-Yon, 1956), 93-141

Cherington, P. T., *The Wool Industry,* (New York, 1916)

Clapham, J.H., *The Woollen and Worsted Industries,* (London, 1907)

Clause, G., 'L'industrie lainière rémoise a l'époque napoléonienne',

Revue d'histoire moderne et contemporaine 17 (1970), 574–95

Colin, A., 'Un siècle de vie lainière à Reims', *Almanach Matot-Brainé* (1937–38)

Crouzet, F., 'French Economic Growth in the Nineteenth Century Reconsidered', *History*, 59 (1974), 167–79

Dieudonné, C., *Statistique du Département du Nord*, (Douai, 1804)

Dunham, A. L., 'The Economic History of France 1815–1870', *Journal of Modern History* 21 (1949), 121–39

Dunham, A. L., *The Industrial Revolution in France 1815–48*, (Ann Arbor, 1955)

Duveau, G., *La Vie ouvrière en France sous le Second Empire*, (Paris, 1946)

Ernouf, Baron A., *Histoire de Quatre Inventeurs Français*, (Paris, 1884)

Exposition Universelle de 1851 à Londres: travaux de la Commission Française, (Paris, 1850)

Falleur, A., *L'Industrie lainière dans la région de Fourmies*, (Paris, 1930)

Fohlen, C., 'Esquisse d'une évolution industrielle: Roubaix au XIXe siècle', *Revue du Nord* 33 (1951), 92–102

Fohlen, C., *L'Industrie textile au temps du Second Empire*, (Paris, 1956)

Fortunes Made in Business, (London, 1884)

France, Catalogue des brevets d'invention, (Paris, 1844–53)

France. Enquête parlementaire sur le régime économique. Industries textiles, vol. II Laine, (Paris, 1870)

France. Ministère de l'agriculture, du commerce, et des travaux publiques, Enquête: Traité de commerce avec l'Angleterre, (Paris, 1860)

France. Ministère de l'industrie et du commerce, Brevets d'invention français, 1791–1902: Un siècle de progrès technique, (Paris, 1958)

France. Ministère du commerce, Enquête sur les fils de laine longue peignée, tordus, du cordonnet et grillée (décembre, 1836), (Paris, 1836)

France. Ministère du commerce, de l'industrie, des postes et télégraphes, etc., Rapport général sur l'industrie française: sa situation, son avenir, (Paris, 1919)

France. Ministère du commerce, de l'industrie, etc., Résultats statistiques du recensement des industries et professions. Dénombrement général de la population du 29 mars 1896, (Paris, 1901)

France, Sénat, Commission d'enquête sur les souffrances du commerce et de l'industrie, (Paris, 1878)

France, Statistique de la France, Industrie, (Paris, 1847–52)

France. Statistique de la France, Industrie. Résultats généraux de l'enquête, 1861–65, (Nancy, 1873)

France. Statistique de la France. Résultats du dénombrement de la population en 1856, (Paris 1856)

France, Statistique de la France, Statistique sommaire des industries principales en 1873, (Paris, 1874)

Franchomme, G., 'L'évolution démographique et économique de Roubaix de 1870 à 1900', *Revue du Nord* 51 (1969), 201-247

Goblet, A., *Le Peignage de la laine à Roubaix-Tourcoing et son évolution économique et sociale*, (Lille, 1903)

Gordon, D. M., 'Merchants and Capitalists: Industrialization and Provincial Politics at Reims and St. Etienne under the Second Republic and Second Empire', Ph.D. dissertation, Brown University (1978)

Gossez, A-M., *Le Département du Nord sous la Seconde République*, (Lille, 1904)

Graham Clark, W. A., *Manufacture of Woolen, Worsted and Shoddy in France and England and Jute in Scotland*, (Washington, 1909)

Grandgeorge, G., *Commission permanente des valeurs de douane: les industries textiles de la France en 1898*, (Paris, 1899)

Hémardinquer, J. J., 'Une dynastie de mécaniciens anglais en France: James, John et Juliana Collier (1791-1847), *Revue d'histoire des sciences et de leurs applications* 17 (1964), 193-208

Henderson, W. O., *Britain and Industrial Europe, 1750-1870*, (Leicester, 1965)

Histoire documentaire de l'industrie de Mulhouse et de ses environs au XIXe siècle, (Mulhouse, 1902)

Hodgson, J., *Textile Manufacture and Other Industries in Keighley*, (Keighley, 1879)

James, J., *The History and Topography of Bradford*, (London, 1841).

Jenkins, D. T. and K. G. Ponting, *The British Wool Textile Industry, 1770-1914*, (London, 1982)

Jennings, E., 'Sir Isaac Holden (1807-1897): "The First Comber in Europe"', Ph. D. dissertation, University of Bradford (1982)

Kahan-Rabecq, M. M., *L'Alsace économique et sociale sous le règne de Louis-Philippe*, (Paris, 1939)

Lambert-Dansette, J., *Quelques familles du patronat textile de Lille-Armentières (1789-1914)*, (Lille, 1954)

Lamoitier, P., *Traité Théorique et Pratique de Tirage, Peignage et Filature de la laine peignée*, (Paris, 1912)

Landes, D., 'Religion and Enterprise: The Case of the French Textile Industry', in E.C. Carter, R. Forster and J.N. Moody, *Enterprise and Entrepreneurs in Nineteenth and Twentieth Century France*, (London, 1976), 41-86

Landes, D., *The Unbound Prometheus*, (Cambridge, 1969)

Lasserrre, A., *La Situation des ouvriers de l'industrie textile dans la région lilloise sous la Monarchie de juillet*, (Lausanne, 1953)

Laurent, G. and G. Boussinesq, *Histoire de Reims depuis les origines jusqu'à nos jours*, (Reims, 1933)

Lazonick, W., 'Industrial Organization and Technological Change: The Decline of the British Cotton Industry', *Business History Review* 57 (1983), 195–236

Lefèvre, E., *Histoire économique de la laine*, (Reims, 1906)

Lefèvre, E., *L'Industrie lainière actuelle*, (Reims, 1912)

Leuridan, T., *Histoire de Roubaix*, (Roubaix, 1859–64)

Lévy-Leboyer, M., *Les Banques européennes et l'industrialisation internationale dans la première moitié du XIXe siècle*, (Paris, 1964)

Lévy-Leboyer, M., 'La croissance économique en France au XIXe siècle', *Annales: E.S.C.* 23 (1968), 788–807

Lister, S. C., *Lord Masham's Inventions: Written by Himself*, (London, 1905)

Markovitch, T. J., 'L'industrie française de 1789 à 1964, *Cahiers de l'ISEA* ser AF 6 (1966)

Marteau, C., *Tableau synoptique de l'industrie lainière, 1789–1900*, (Reims, 1900)

Mathias, P., 'Skills and the Diffusion of Innovation from Britain in the Eighteenth Century', *Transactions of the Royal Historical Society* 25 (1975), 93–113

Milward, A. S. and S. B. Saul, *The Economic Development of Continental Europe, 1780–1870*, (London, 1979)

Monin, H., *Histoire de la ville de Saint-Denis et de la Basilique*, (Paris, 1928)

Morazé, P., 'The Treaty of 1860 and the Industry of the Department of the North', *Economic History Review* 10 (1939–40), 18–28

Moreau-Berillon, C., *Le Mouton en Champagne*, (Paris, 1909)

Mussault, M., 'Histoire du marché à terme en laines peignées de Roubaix-Tourcoing', Thèse de droit, Paris (1909)

Nicol, J. F., 'L'industrialisation de la commune de St. Denis dans la seconde moitié du 19e siècle', Thèse maitresse, Université de Paris X (1972)

Noble, D., *America by Design*, (Oxford, 1979)

Le Nord Industriel, 'Les Pionniers' Special Supplement, (June, 1966)

P. O'Brien and C. Keyder, *Economic Growth in Britain and France, 1780–1914*, (London, 1978)

Paris. Chambre de Commerce, *Statistique de l'industrie à Paris, résultant de l'enquête par la Chambre de Commerce de Paris pour les années 1847–1848*, (Paris, 1851)

Paris. Exposition des produits de l'industrie, *Rapport du Jury Central sur les produits de l'industrie française exposés en 1834*, (Paris, 1836)

Paris. Exposition des produits de l'industrie, *Exposition des produits de l'industrie française en 1839: Rapport du Jury Central*, (Paris, 1839)

Paris. Exposition des produits de l'industrie, *Rapport du Jury Central des produits de l'agriculture et de l'industrie exposés en 1849*, (Paris, 1850)

Picard, A., *Le Bilan d'un siècle, 1801–1900*, (Paris, 1906)

Penrose, E., *The Economics of the International Patent System*, (Baltimore, 1951)

Perrot, M., *Les Ouvriers en Grève*, (Paris, 1974)

Piat, J., *Croix: Dix Siècles d'Histoire*, (Croix, 1972)

Pollard, S., *Peaceful Conquest: The Industrialization of Europe, 1760–1970*, (Oxford, 1981)

Price, R., *The Economic Modernisation of France*, (London, 1975)

Priestman, H., *Principles of Wool Combing*, (London, 1921)

Raman, M., 'Mesure de la croissance d'un centre textile: Roubaix de 1789 à 1913' *Revue d'histoire économique et sociale* 51 (1973), 470–501

Reybaud, L., *La Laine*, (Paris, 1867)

Rimmer, B. M., *Guide to Industrial Property Literature: France*, (London, 1980)

Rosenberg, N. (ed.), *The Economics of Technological Change*, (Harmondsworth, 1971)

Rosenberg, N., *Inside the Black Box*, (Cambridge, 1983)

Rosenberg, N., *Perspectives on Technology*, (Cambridge, 1976)

Roehl, R., 'French Industrialization: A Reconsideration', *Explorations in Economic History* 13 (1976), 233–281

Saul, S. B., 'The Nature and Diffusion of Technology', in A. J., Youngson, *Economic Development in the Long Run*, (London, 1972), 36–61

Sigsworth, E.M., 'Sir Isaac Holden, Bt.: The first comber in Europe', in N.B. Harte and K.G. Ponting (eds.), *Textile History and Economic History*, (Manchester, 1973), 339–353.

Sigsworth, E.M., *Black Dyke Mills*, (Liverpool, 1958).

Stearns, P.N., 'Individualism and Association in French Industry, 1820–1848', *Business History Review* 40 (1966), 297–320.

Stearns, P.N., *Paths to Authority*, (Urbana, 1978).

Subject Matter Index. Patents for Inventions Granted in France from 1791 to 1876 inclusive, (Washington, 1883).

Tilly, L.A., 'The Family Wage Economy of a French Textile City: Roubaix, 1872–1906', *Journal of Family History* (Winter, 1979), 381–94.

Tricket, J.M., 'A Technological Appraisal of the Isaac Holden Papers', M. Sc. dissertation, University of Bradford (1977).

Turgan, J., *Les Grandes usines, études industrielles en France et l'étranger*, (Paris, 1866–89).

United Kingdom. Foreign Office, *Consular Reports*.

United Kingdom. *Second Report of the Royal Commission on Technical Instruction*, Parliamentary Papers XXIV vol. I (1884), 249–61.

United Kingdom. Committee on Industry and Trade, *Survey of Industries*, (London, 1928).

US Department of State. Commercial Relations of the United States, *Cotton and Woolen Mills in Europe. Report from the Consuls of the US, 23 September 1882*, (Washington, 1882).

Vaughan, F.L., 'Patent Policy', *American Economic Review: Papers and Proceedings* 38 (1948), 215-34.

Vaughan, F.L., *The United States Patent System*, (Norman, Okla., 1956).

Index